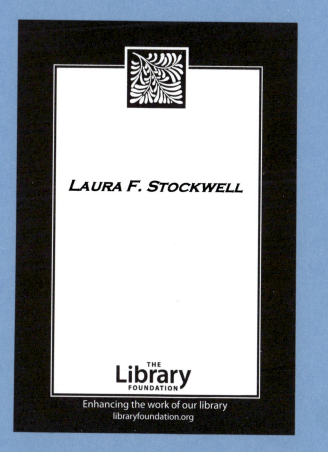

To my mother, who launched me with a prenatal ice cream diet.

Published in 2013 by Stewart, Tabori & Chang

An imprint of ABRAMS

Copyright © 2013 Jennie Schacht

Photographs copyright © 2013 Sara Remington, except image on page 10, courtesy of Shorpy.com

Cataloging-in-Publication Data has been applied for and may be obtained from the Library of Congress.

ISBN: 978-1-61769-036-5

Editor: Elinor Hutton
Food Stylist: Kim Kissling
Prop Stylist: Dani Fisher
Designer: Modern Good
Production Manager: Anet Sirna-Bruder

The text of this book was composed in Berthold Akzidenz Grotesk and Century Schoolbook.

Printed and bound in the United States of America

10 9 8 7 6 5 4 3 2 1

Stewart, Tabori & Chang books are available at special discounts when purchased in quantity for premiums and promotions as well as fundraising or educational use. Special editions can also be created to specification. For details, contact specialsales@abramsbooks.com or the address below.

THE ART OF BOOKS SINCE 1949

115 West 18th Street
New York, NY 10011
www.abramsbooks.com

I SCREAM

INSPIRED RECIPES FOR THE ULTIMATE FROZEN TREAT

SANDWICH!

Jennie Schacht

PHOTOGRAPHS BY Sara Remington

STEWART, TABORI & CHANG

NEW YORK

i scream SANDWICH!

More reassuring than a cupcake. More enticing than a petite French macaron. More retro than a whoopie pie. It's that childhood favorite whose allure never fades, even into adulthood—the ice cream sandwich, pure delight in portable packaging.

The ice cream sandwich is iconic. It says comfort and ecstasy in every bite. It is cold but makes you feel warm inside. An ice cream sandwich is the dessert you pulled from the vending machine after an invigorating childhood swim at the local pool, and the one you look for now at your local creamery. Served in its own neat little package, it provides the gooey-creamy-messy satisfaction of the best desserts as it melts.

I got my start making ice cream sandwiches years ago, when I offered to make a friend's birthday dessert. His wife suggested fudge brownies topped with mint chocolate chip ice cream, his favorite. I had to go one better, so I combined the two in a mint chocolate chip brownie ice cream sandwich (page 148). The seductive squares have so often been requested since that day that they now make regular appearances at occasions ranging from casual movie nights to major holidays. Soon, I began improving on Jon's favorite by making my own mint chip ice cream, using mint from my garden with a boost from peppermint oil.

After tinkering with ice cream flavors and holders, I became obsessed with discovering new combinations of texture and flavor, from cookies to bars, mix-ins and roll-'ems, dairy and non-dairy ice creams, even venturing into cakes and breads after discovering *brioche con gelato*—ice cream served in a brioche roll—while traveling in Sicily.

With a favorite scoop sandwiched between two edible book-ends, the dessert lends itself to infinite variation. Now, just about any cookie, cake, or pie makes me wonder how it could be reimagined as a sandwich, and I've worked out all sorts of sauces, toppings, and garnishes to mix, match, and embellish them. This book is meant to get you started on your exploration, with creative, satisfying combinations and plenty of tools and inspiration to spark your own creations.

The recipes offer the do-it-yourselfer the opportunity to make both the ice cream and cookies from scratch, and homemade is the ticket to the very best sandwiches. However, you'll also find plenty of shortcuts for embellishing store-bought ice cream with simple mix-ins, using ready-bake or store-bought holders, or both. No matter your skill level, no matter how busy your schedule, there is plenty here for you. I mean, any-one can make a sandwich, right? It need be no more difficult than scooping ice cream and pressing it between cookies.

What I love about these sandwiches is that they are versatile enough to fit any occasion. I always keep a few sandwiches in the freezer to satisfy late-afternoon ice cream cravings, or for drop-in guests. As a thank-you to helpful neighbors and friends, I might stop by with a couple of sandwiches packed into waxed paper bags. We enjoy them on the sofa in front of the television, serve them at barbecues and around the picnic table, and deck them out for special occasions. They are fantastic for entertaining, as most of the sandwiches allow you to make the components and assemble the sandwiches ahead, whisking out your finished desserts at the appointed time. Cut into cute shapes with cookie cutters or molds, they are perfect for children's birthday parties. For an adult party, try making (or purchasing) a variety of ice creams, cookies, and toppings, setting them out to let everyone come up with their own combinations. You could even have a contest for the most creative, outrageous, beautiful, or delicious sandwich.

A brief history of the ice cream sandwich

Legend has it the ice cream sandwich originated in 1899, in the pushcarts of lower Manhattan's Bowery. A July 1900 article in the *Washington Post* describes them: "The ice cream sandwich man, who sells quarter-inch layers of alleged ice cream between tiny slabs of water wafers, did a big business during the hot spell. His field of operation was within the district inhabited by the Russians, and his pushcart was elaborately decorated with signs in Hebrew characters. He made the sandwiches quickly in a tin mold, and was kept so busy that he could not make change, but insisted on receiving the actual price for each ice cream sandwich—1 cent." Alleged ice cream? Water wafers? I'll take a scoop of homemade ice cream between two soft, chewy cookies, thank you very much.

Another article that year describes sandwiches made on a graham wafer (getting better, no?), selling for two or three cents, and attracting "a jostling, sweltering crowd of patrons, representing all social conditions, from banker down to bootblack and newsboy." Apparently that price hike caused such a commotion the vendors were forced to drop the price back to a penny. By 1905, the carts were appearing outside of New York City, and a trend was born.

More elaborate variations soon sprouted up. In 1928, George Whitney began a San Francisco tradition when he sandwiched vanilla ice cream between two oatmeal cookies and dipped the whole thing in chocolate, creating the It's-It, sold exclusively at San Francisco's Playland at the Beach for more than forty years. The treat is now distributed throughout the Western states and has been called San Francisco's official food. (You'll find my version on page 41.)

Then there's the Chipwich: a packaged ice cream novelty between two cookies, originally vanilla on chocolate chip. As the company's website tells the story, the Chipwich folks were the first to sell a chocolate chip cookie ice cream sandwich, and it quickly overtook all other treats in the small shop where it was first made. The sandwich was named through a contest, and apparently the moniker was quite successful: The company thanked the young student who submitted the winning name by putting her through college. You can make your own version using my Milk and Cookies recipe (page 114)—one of the simplest in the book.

In Maine, the Harbor Bar is made by coating soft chocolate chip cookies filled with vanilla ice cream in chocolate—you could do the same using the chocolate chip cookies on page 115, and the ice cream and dipping instructions in the Better-Than-It on page 41. In 1945, Pennsylvania's Jerry Newberg was selling slices of vanilla ice cream sandwiched between two rectangular chocolate wafers at Forbes Field, former home of the Pittsburgh Pirates—a combination that remains a time-tested favorite, and the inspiration for my Pure Nostalgia sandwich (page 30).

Versions of the ice cream sandwich can be found around the globe. There's the Giant Sandwich in Australia, also akin to the Pure Nostalgia. In New Zealand, they sell the biscuits (pink ones!) and ice cream together but packaged separately so you can put them together yourself. The soft, yeasted bread called *pandesal* is used for making ice cream sandwiches in the Philippines, much like Sicilian Breakfast (page 119)—gelato tucked into a brioche bun—but using local ice cream flavors like purple yam. In Singapore, the holder of choice is a wafer, which is used to make what the locals call a *phia*, or biscuit ice cream sandwich. The ice cream is sometimes tucked into bread there too. In Scotland, you might find a nougat wafer: ice cream between two rectangular waffle cookies, each filled with nougat, the sides coated in chocolate. It's a lot to get your mouth around. Order sliders in Northern Ireland and you may get ice cream sandwiched similarly between nougat wafers, or between a plain wafer and a nougat wafer.

A perennial favorite, the ice cream sandwich has remained in high demand since it was introduced. There's even a day dedicated to it in the United States: August 2 is said to be Ice Cream Sandwich Day. These days, the treat seems to have come full circle, rediscovering its Bowery roots on the modern-day equivalent of its birthplace: the food truck.

How to use this book

The two chapters that follow provide a thorough orientation to making, freezing, constructing, and serving ice cream sandwiches, including key ingredients, tools, and techniques.

In the recipes throughout the book, the filling and holder headings in the ingredient lists display symbols to indicate those recipes that are gluten-free (GF) and/or dairy-free (DF), making these easy to spot. You can also find these recipes listed in the index. These icons are not meant as medical or nutritional advice. There is a great deal of variation in manufacturing processes that may affect the ingredients you use. Consult the manufacturer to determine whether their products are certified gluten or dairy free and, if you have health concerns or are on a restricted diet, seek appropriate medical and nutritional advice.

Each sandwich recipe includes suggestions for substitutions and embellishments:

- **Take it easy** shows tips for substituting store-bought ingredients, with suggestions for adding flavorings and mix-ins to make them similar to the recipes.

- **Dress it up** includes options for adding mix-ins or spreads, rolling the sides of the sandwiches in nuts or other goodies, or dipping them in sauces or coatings.

While I've shared my cream-of-the-crop collection of sandwiches in this book, I hope you won't stop there. **Sandwich It Your Way!** (page 166) provides a chart to get you started creating your own combinations.

Now, stop that screaming—let's make i scream SANDWICHes!

Chapter

Sandwich Secrets

I know too many people who love to cook but are afraid to bake. I have good news: It doesn't take training as a pastry chef to bring forth creamy, intensely flavored ice creams from your ice cream maker, or to bake cookies ready to sandwich into tantalizing frozen morsels. This chapter tells you all you need to produce sandwiches that are as captivating to eat as they are to look at.

Ice cream

is not nearly so temperamental as many other kinds of baking and pastry products. These recipes are reasonably foolproof, in part because they are well tested, but also because they tend to be less exacting, with room for error. Making these sandwiches is all about fun. Throw a sandwich-making party with friends and you will up the fun factor exponentially. When sandwiching ice cream between layers of cookies, brownies, or other good things, it's hard to go wrong.

That said, there are a few things you can do to assure supple ice cream free of icy crystals, and cookies with a pleasing chew or crunch when frozen. In this chapter, I share tips and tricks for making the most of your frozen beauties, including how to make great ice cream, the characteristics of the best sandwich holders, and a guide to putting the two together. In the next chapter, we'll drill down into details of ingredients and equipment that contribute to the best sandwiches. It won't be long before you're a pro.

What makes a great i scream SANDWICH!?

Ice cream sandwiches are all about contrast: a creamy or frosty center against a chewy or crisp holder, with complementary flavors to seal the deal. There may be additional contrast when the filling is frozen and the holder is at room temperature, or even warmed. These recipes combine flavors ranging from the familiar to the unique, in combinations that please and sometimes surprise, but never disappoint.

The combination of several important qualities works to make an ideal sandwich. It goes without saying that you've got to start with great-tasting ingredients, but there's more to it than that. The filling should be full-flavored and either silky smooth or, in the case of sorbets, composed of fine ice crystals that readily melt on the tongue. It must be supple, but not so soft that it oozes

out when you bite through the cookie. The cookies may be crisp, chewy, crumbly, or soft, but they must be well matched to the filling. For soft and chewy cookies, and most brownies and bars, we'll be slightly underbaking them for the best consistency when frozen.

Keys to great ice creams, ice milks, sorbets, and sherbets

A great ice cream sandwich filling must be firm enough to hold up to the cookies or other holders without squishing out the sides, yet not so firm that you can't easily bite into it. To achieve that balance, I use specific ingredients that enhance creaminess without making the ice cream overly soft and melty. A splash of alcohol occasionally helps, and though sugar keeps ice cream from freezing hard, I'd rather not drown the flavor of my ice cream in excess sweetness. We have better ways. In engineering these recipes, I've found the most effective tools to lock up water that could turn to hard ice crystals are tapioca starch and inverted sugar syrup, or sometimes other syrups. Sorbets and non-dairy frozen desserts are always icier, but the ice is fine rather than coarse, part of their refreshing appeal. We'll learn more about these and other key ingredients in the next chapter.

To make the creamiest ice cream in a home ice cream maker, be sure to **have everything as chilly as possible** before spinning. I quickly cool the ice cream mixture in an ice bath, refrigerate it until cold, and, finally, slip it into the freezer before spinning; avoid letting it freeze hard. If time is short, I skip the refrigerator and go directly from ice bath to freezer, letting it chill there until it turns icy around the edges only, about two hours, stirring occasionally for uniform chilling. When using the type of machine with an insulated bowl, get the bowl into the freezer 24 hours in advance. (Until my obsession forced me to step up to the compressor-freezer ice cream maker

model, mine lived there.) While the base chills, put the ice cream maker's dasher and cover into the freezer too, along with a container for packing the finished ice cream, and a spatula.

When you're ready to spin the ice cream, if possible, **pour the ice cream mixture in a slow stream into the running machine** to begin freezing it quickly as it hits the machine's cold walls. **Process the ice cream a little longer than you think is needed** for maximum smoothness and volume.

Listen up! The ice cream is done when it wraps around the dasher and stays there, moving as a block rather than flowing around the dasher. If you perk up your ears, you will hear the sound drop to a deeper register as the dasher works harder to move the thickened ice cream, a hint to check if it is ready.

Using store-bought ice cream

Most of the recipes include options for swapping store-bought ice cream for homemade. For many of these, you can just scoop it between two cookies. For recipes that shape the ice cream, if it came in a cardboard container, slice it right through the cardboard using a serrated knife, then use cookie cutters to cut out shapes to fit your cookies. You can also slightly soften the ice cream, then spread it about ¾ inch (2 cm) thick on a baking sheet or in a freezer-safe pan lined with parchment or waxed paper, pressing plastic wrap over the top to evenly smooth the surface. Freeze the ice cream until firm, about 4 hours, then use cutters or molds to shape the ice cream.

Sandwich math

For most recipes, the cookies make the exact number needed for the recipe, and the filling a bit more than needed, allowing for variation in scoop sizes. Keep in mind that sampling as you cook, chill, and pack your ice cream will dwindle away your yield, possibly leaving you short.

For the typical 12 sandwiches, each filled with ¼ to ⅓ cup (60 to 80 ml) of ice cream, you will need 24 cookies and 3 to 4 cups (720 to 960 ml) of ice cream. The recipes in this book typically make 1 quart (1L), which should be more than enough to fill 12 sandwiches. If you come up short on cookies, consider making some of the sandwiches open-faced—they're quite adorable, and as we were testing, some tasters requested their sandwiches that way. (These can be stored ice-cream-side up in a parchment-lined airtight container but are not suitable for individual wrapping.) Enjoy leftover ice cream by the scoop. If you make several different sandwiches, you'll have the fixings for a Banana Split sandwich party (page 129), with lots of leftover ice creams and toppings to mix and match.

Timing

Although the recipes have many steps, each step is reasonably quick and easy. (My testers, who are home cooks, agree!) Tackle the sandwiches in pieces as your time allows, or use the suggested store-bought substitutes to save time. (If you do have the time, the homemade versions are yardsticks beyond anything you can buy.) Be sure to read through the entire recipe and plan ahead so you won't be disappointed by not having the sandwiches ready when you need them. Here's the most efficient way to approach the recipes:

1. For most of the sandwiches, **make the ice cream first**—either early in the day or, better yet, the day before you plan to complete the sandwiches. You'll need time to chill the mixture

before spinning it and, for most, additional time (6 hours or more) after spinning to firm up the ice cream before assembling.

2. **Bake the cookies while the ice cream mixture chills, spins, or firms in the freezer.**

3. Be sure to **have any ripples or mix-ins at room temperature or colder** for mixing into the just-made ice cream without melting it.

4. Many of the sandwiches may be served immediately after filling or can be frozen ahead. Sandwiches made in a large block are **best filled the night before**, allowing time to become quite firm for easily cutting into bars.

5. Sandwiches that have been frozen ahead are **best enjoyed slightly thawed**; just 5 to 10 minutes at room temperature transforms a rock-hard sandwich into creamy ice cream encased in pleasingly soft, chewy, cakey, or flaky cookies or bars.

Using cutters and molds

Molds and cutters (page 23) can be fun and helpful for cutting cookies into uniform shapes, and for assembling the cookies and ice cream into sharp-looking, neat, and adorable sandwiches. Consider scalloped or plain round cookie cutters, or ones in heart, leaf, gingerbread man, ice cream (cone, sundae, or bar), or holiday shapes. Some cutters are not sufficiently sharp to cut fresh-from-the-oven cookies, so I sometimes cut around them with a paring knife for a clean edge. If you don't have the right size cutter for the ice cream, try an overturned drinking glass with the right diameter.

Asymmetrical cutters will cause mismatched cookies. Remedy this by cutting half of the cookies with the cutter inverted to form a mirror image, then pair the cookies so that they match with bottom sides together.

Storing your SANDWICH!es

For short-term storage, leave the sandwiches layered between sheets of parchment or waxed paper in the container in which you packed them.

For longer storage, to maintain their shape and flavor, individually wrap sandwiches in plastic wrap or waxed paper, or slip them into small waxed paper or cellophane bags, and freeze in an airtight container or zipper-top bag. Sandwiches requiring last-minute assembly, or that do not store well, are noted in the recipes.

Bear in mind that the filled sandwiches will continue to evolve in the freezer over time, often for the better. If you make a batch of sandwiches and taste them day after day, as I did while developing this book, you may find that some flavors become more intense and others more muted. Textures may change too, with many of the cookies, ribbons, and swirls softening over time in contact with the filling. To me, these changes are all charming and interesting, but if consistency and perfection are important to you, you may wish to serve the sandwiches within a day or two of making them. In developing and testing the sandwiches, I ate some that had been in the freezer for several weeks and they were still thoroughly enjoyable. Well wrapped, most should keep for up to one month.

Assembling the sandwiches

I use four basic assembly methods, each detailed here: rustic style, using cookie cutters or molds, making matching cookie and ice cream cut-outs, and forming the sandwiches in slabs and cutting them into bars. While each recipe indicates a preferred method, most may be adapted to others, by using cutters or molds instead of pressing the ice cream between two cookies, for example, or by baking the cookies in a slab and cutting them into bars.

For all assembly methods, **cool the cookies or bars completely before sandwiching.** (Please note that some methods have you cut the cookies before cooling.) Have the **ice cream firm but slightly softened:** Transfer the container to the refrigerator for about 20 minutes, or to the countertop for about 10 minutes. **Have ready one or more airtight containers** large enough to hold all of the finished sandwiches, and pieces of waxed paper or parchment paper to layer between them. As you form the sandwiches, transfer them to the prepared container, returning the container to the freezer each time you complete a layer. Transfer leftover ice cream to an airtight container, press plastic wrap directly over the surface, cover, and freeze.

Rustic Sandwiches

1. Pair the cookies with like-size mates.
2. Place a ¼-cup (60-ml) scoop of ice cream (⅓ cup / 80 ml for large cookies, ice cream quantity permitting) between the bottoms of each cookie pair. For the neatest scoops, use a measuring cup with straight sides, about the diameter of the cookies, to measure out the ice cream. Fill the measure according to the recipe, and use a knife or offset spatula to release the scoop onto a cookie bottom.
3. Press gently to squeeze the ice cream slightly beyond the edge of the cookies. If desired, use a small offset spatula or the flat side of a dinner knife to smooth the ice cream flush with the edge.

Using Ice Cream Sandwich Molds or Cookie Cutters as Molds

1. Select an ice cream sandwich mold or a 2- to 3-inch (5- to 7½-cm) cutter that is about 2 inches (5 cm) high. (A round biscuit cutter works well.) Whether you baked the cookies in a slab or individually, slide the just-baked cookies on their liner to a flat surface, then immediately cut out the cookies with cutters. (In the case of individual cookies, you will be using the cutters to neatly trim them.)
2. Lay a piece of waxed paper on a flat surface to catch drips and place the cutter on top of it. Place one pre-cut cookie top-side down into the cutter so that it lies flat against the paper. Scoop ¼ to ⅓ cup (60 to 80 ml) of ice cream (quantity permitting) into the cutter over the cookie.
3. Top with a second cookie, top-side up, and use the mold's plunger to firmly press the cookie over the ice cream and compact the filling. If using a cookie cutter, use a drinking

glass or flat-bottomed bottle that fits inside the cutter as a plunger to press the top cookie onto the filling. Continue pressing the plunger while lifting the cutter or mold to release the sandwich.

Making Cookie and Ice Cream Cutouts

1. Transfer the ice cream directly from the ice cream machine into a 13-by-9-inch (33-by-23-cm) pan lined with waxed paper or parchment paper extending up two sides as a sling for easy removal. Cover the ice cream with plastic wrap, pressing it directly against the surface, and freeze until quite firm, at least 6 hours.
2. Select 2- to 3-inch (5- to 7½-cm) cutters, using one or more shapes. Whether you baked the cookies in a slab or individually, slide the just-baked cookies on their liner to a flat surface, then immediately cut out the cookies with cutters. (In the case of individual cookies, you will be using the cutters to neatly trim them.)
3. Remove the ice cream from the freezer and use the sling to lift it from the pan to a flat surface, cutting around the edges with a knife to loosen it, if needed.
4. Use the same cutter(s) used for the cookies to cut matching shapes from the ice cream, cutting as many shapes as you have sets of cookies, and gathering scraps to form the last few shapes, if needed. As you make them, use a small offset spatula to slide the ice cream cutouts between two cookie bottoms.

Using Brownie or Cookie Slabs to Form Bars

1. Bake brownies, cookies, bars, or slabs, using two 8- or 9-inch (20- or 23-cm) square pans, or one 13-by-9-inch (33-by-23-cm) pan, or as directed in the recipe. (Be sure to line the pan(s) with parchment paper extending up two sides as a sling for easy removal.)
2. Use the sling to remove the cooled slab(s) from the pan(s), cutting around the edges of the pan with a knife to loosen, if needed. For a 13-by-9-inch (33-by-23-cm) pan, cut the large slab in half to form two 9-by-6½ inch (23-by-16½-cm) rectangles. Wrap the slabs in plastic and freeze until the ice cream is ready.
3. Form the sandwich block in the pan used to bake the brownie or bar, or on a baking sheet. (If you used a 13-by-9-inch / 33-by-23-cm pan, you will be filling only half the pan.) Line the pan or sheet with plastic wrap, extending it well beyond the edges on all four sides.
4. Place one slab top-side down in the pan and spread softened ice cream over it in an even layer. Top with the second slab, top-side up, pressing firmly to evenly distribute the ice cream. Wrap tightly in the plastic wrap and freeze until very firm, at least 6 hours or overnight, for easiest cutting.
5. When the ice cream is very firm, take the pan from the freezer, remove and unwrap the block, and place it on a flat cutting surface. Use a sharp, heavy knife to cut the block following recipe instructions, dipping the knife in hot water and wiping it dry between cuts.

Chapter 2

Essential Equipment, Ingredients, and Building Block Recipes

Only a few special ingredients and tools are needed to produce the best ice cream sandwiches, most of them amenable to substitutions. The most critical is an ice cream machine, though it is possible to make ice cream without one; I've included a few easy methods. You'll also find building block recipes used throughout the book: inverted sugar syrup, strained yogurt, and crème fraîche. Sources for ingredients and equipment are included in Sources and Resources, beginning on page 168.

Essential Equipment

Ice cream machines.

I used three machines for making the ice creams in this book: the Cuisinart ICE-20 and the KitchenAid ice cream bowl attachment—both of which require freezing an insulated bowl overnight (I suggest 24 hours)—and the Whynter SNO (IC-2L), a 2-quart compressor-freezer model that generates its own cold (and you just can't beat that name). All three work well and produce similar results: soft-serve ice creams and sorbets without excessive air that become firm after a few hours in the freezer. (Compressor-freezer models are considerably more costly.)

Cuisinart makes probably the most commonly used ice cream maker in home kitchens. My ICE-20 takes about 25 minutes to spin 1 quart (960 ml) of ice cream, and the ICE-21 that replaced it is said to complete the task in 15 to 20 minutes. Some say they are able to squeeze in a second batch before the coolant in the bowl has thawed, but I am skeptical—I think this type of machine works best with a fully frozen bowl. Cuisinart also makes compressor-freezer models.

The KitchenAid attachment works similarly to the Cuisinart except that it takes the place of your mixer bowl, using the stand mixer's motor to turn the dasher. You won't need to store a separate machine, though the bowl takes up slightly more freezer space (and has a larger capacity: 2 quarts, versus 1½ for the Cuisinart). I found it fast and effective. (Disclosure: KitchenAid provided the attachment for my evaluation as I prepared the manuscript for this book.)

The Whynter is the slowest of the three, taking about 40 minutes to spin 1 quart (960 ml) of ice cream. It takes up more counter space but no freezer space, and it freezes batches of ice cream back to back without waiting for a canister to freeze. I can't imagine how we would have turned out the forty batches needed for our photo shoot without this workhorse. One small gripe: The feed tube is too small for adding most mix-ins; you'll have to do it by hand as you pack the ice cream into a container, which really isn't much trouble.

A number of companies produce machines that use a tub inside an outer bucket you fill with ice and rock salt. In most, a motor powers the dasher; a few use a hand crank, like the Sears version I grew up with. These machines are larger and clunkier than the freezer bowl–style machines, but don't require you to freeze a bowl and are less costly than the compressor-style machines. They also tend to have a larger capacity.

No ice cream maker? No problem!

It is well worth investing in an ice cream machine if you plan to make ice cream more than a few times. Even the least expensive models generally do a very good job. However, in a pinch, there are a number of ways to make ice cream without one by keeping the mixture in constant motion as it freezes. As with the machines, these methods make ice cream with a soft-serve texture; quickly transfer the ice cream to an airtight container and allow extra time to freeze before sandwiching.

Even more so than with the machines, you will want to get your mixture as icy cold as possible before starting the freezing process. Freeze the mixture in an airtight container for about an hour before you begin, but avoid letting it freeze solid.

For a simple sorbet, process chunks of ripe frozen fruits in a blender with inverted sugar syrup (page 27) and lemon juice to taste and freeze until firm. A tablespoon of alcohol (gin, vodka, rum, tequila) per pint of sorbet will help prevent it from freezing rock hard.

To simulate an ice cream maker, chill the ice cream mixture in a heavy-duty zipper-top bag with a reliable seal. Nestle the sealed bag inside a larger zipper-top bag filled with ice and rock salt. Tightly seal the outer bag, then shake, toss, or roll the two together until the ice cream freezes to a soft-serve consistency. Quickly transfer the inner bag to the freezer until firm. (You can freeze the slushy ice-salt mixture in the large bag for future batches of ice cream.)

You can accomplish roughly the same thing by putting the ice cream mixture in a metal bowl nested inside a larger bowl filled with ice and rock salt, the ice coming up the sides to the level of the ice cream mixture. Holding the inner bowl firmly to avoid spills, use a handheld electric mixer on low speed to mix the ice cream until it has the texture of soft-serve, about 20 minutes.

Baking mats and parchment paper.

Silicone baking mats prevent sticking and can be quickly wiped clean, then left in a warm oven to dry and reuse, reducing waste. Parchment is also convenient and is sometimes preferred. Both are a better choice than nonstick baking sheets, which can yield uneven results.

Baking sheets.

Use heavy-gauge aluminum baking sheets to avoid buckling. Rimmed sheets keep ingredients from tumbling over the edges. Most often, I use a rimmed, 17-by-12-inch (43-by-30½-cm) half-sheet pan. For some recipes, a rimless baking sheet is useful for easily sliding baked cookies on their liners onto a wire rack to cool, or onto a flat surface to cut while still warm. Some cookies will brown more quickly on baking sheets with a dark finish; watch carefully and reduce the oven temperature if your cookies brown too quickly. Especially in the case of chewy cookies, you will generally want to slightly underbake for optimal texture when frozen.

Bench scraper.

This straight-edged, broad, stainless-steel blade with a wood, rolled metal, or molded plastic handle is a helpful aide when rolling and cutting dough, gathering up and moving ingredients, and scraping flour or sticky bits from a cutting or rolling surface.

Electric mixer.

A stand mixer is the best tool for mixing ingredients that require more time than you wish to hold a handheld mixer, such as for marshmallows. The paddle attachment is perfect for creaming butter, and the whisk attachment easily whips up fluffy egg whites or cream. If you don't own a stand mixer, a good handheld electric mixer will handle most tasks.

Graters and zesters.

Modeled after a woodworker's rasp, Microplane graters and zesters make easy work of finely shaving the zest from citrus fruits, capturing the flavorful outer layer and avoiding the bitter pith below. They are also useful for grating chocolate.

Ice cream sandwich molds.

Only a few companies make molds used specifically for making ice cream sandwiches (see Sources and Resources, page 168), and they typically include instructions for using them. On page 18 you will find a general method, plus a nifty method for using a biscuit cutter or other tall cutter as a mold to build your sandwiches in neat little packages.

Immersion blender.

This may be my single favorite kitchen tool because it saves me from having to drag out the blender or food processor, instead blending the mixture directly in the saucepan.

Kitchen scale.

Perhaps the most important piece of baking and cooking advice I can share is this: *Weigh rather than measure whenever possible.* Measuring cups are notoriously inaccurate, fickle in size, and subject to great variation in measurements depending on user technique. For reliable results, professional bakers always weigh their ingredients. I prefer an electronic scale that displays both ounces and grams and has a removable platform for easy cleaning, but any scale will do the job, assuming it is accurate and calibrated.

Saucepans.

For heating and thickening ice cream mixtures, use heavy saucepans made of nonreactive material such as anodized aluminum or stainless steel. To avoid discoloration and off flavors from reactions with ingredients, stay away from nonanodized aluminum and cast iron. Light-colored saucepans are best for observing color changes in mixtures that darken, such as caramel.

Scoops.

These handy tools come in a wide range of sizes and are helpful not only for scooping ice cream, but also for uniformly scooping cookie dough. The two I used most often for this book are a spring-loaded 1-tablespoon scoop, for portioning cookie dough, and a ¼-cup (60-ml) scoop, for filling sandwiches.

Spatulas.

The piece of kitchen equipment I reach for most often is one of the least expensive: a small metal **offset spatula**, the kind with a bend in the blade. I use this tool for spreading batter in pans, smoothing the edges of sandwiches, transferring cookies to cooling racks and ice cream cut-outs to the freezer, and a million other tasks. A large, wide spatula is helpful for moving brownies and bars. (A small rimless baking sheet also works well.)

For scraping the sides of mixing bowls, folding ingredients, and heating ice cream mixtures on the stovetop as they thicken, use flexible, **heat-resistant or heatproof silicone spatulas**, available in a variety of sizes. I always have one narrow, one standard, and one spoon-shaped spatula close at hand.

Whisks.

A **large balloon whisk** is the best tool for incorporating air quickly and efficiently into egg whites and other mixtures by hand. A **flat whisk** is perfect for stirring loose batters and ice cream mixtures to remove lumps, before switching to a heatproof spatula.

Essential Ingredients

Most ingredients in this book will be familiar, or are well described in headnotes. A few deserve a bit more detail.

Chocolate and cocoa powder.

Many good brands of **chocolate** are available, including Callebaut, Divine (a fair trade product), El Rey, Guittard (and their E. Guittard line), Michel Cluizel, and Valrhona. Chocolate chips are made to hold their shape when baked and are best saved for cookies unless specified in a recipe.

There is no standardized distinction between bittersweet and semisweet chocolate. When I call for bittersweet chocolate, I mean one with a cacao content ranging from 60 to 70 percent, or occasionally extra bittersweet, from 64 to 72 percent. For semisweet, look for chocolate labeled 50 to 59 percent cacao.

Cocoa powder is chocolate that has had most of its cocoa butter removed before being ground to a powder. Among my favorite brands are Guittard and Penzeys. Some people prefer Dutch-processed (alkalized) cocoa for its dark color and mellow flavor, while others like the pure chocolate flavor of natural cocoa. When baking, use the type of cocoa specified in the recipe as they react differently with leavening. When the cocoa won't be baked, such as in ice cream or fudge ripple, use whatever type you prefer.

Coconut milk.

Coconut milk comes in two types: the one in aseptic boxes found either on grocery shelves near the soy and almond milks or in the refrigerator case, and the type in cans. For either, choose unsweetened, unflavored varieties for the recipes in this book. Do *not* substitute coconut water or sweetened coconut cream, such as Coco Lopez. Full-fat canned coconut milk is preferred in these recipes; I like Mae Ploy, said to be one of the richest, and Chaokoh close behind.

Milk and cream.

For the best results, use fresh, best-quality milk and cream. For heavy (also called heavy whipping) cream, use one that is free of additives or emulsifiers and is not ultrapasteurized. Most recipes call for whole milk, though some offer lower fat options.

Nuts.

The oil in nuts makes them easily go rancid. For the freshest nuts, I store mine in the freezer, which also helps prevent them from turning into a paste when grinding them.

Toast nuts on a rimmed baking sheet in a preheated 350°F (175°C) oven until they are fragrant and golden, 8 to 12 minutes, depending on the variety. (Frozen nuts will take a few minutes longer.) When you bite into one, it should be light tan at the center. For small quantities (less than a cup), if you don't already have the oven on, toast the nuts in a dry skillet over medium-low heat, watching carefully and stirring occasionally to prevent burning. Quickly transfer the toasted nuts to a heatproof surface to cool. Wrap hazelnuts warm from the oven in a terry cloth dish towel and rub vigorously to remove most of their skins.

Salt.

Most recipes call for kosher salt. Look for a brand with no additives to impart chemical or other harsh flavors. Fine sea salt also has a clean taste and dissolves easily. (When substituting fine salt, use half the amount of kosher salt called for in the recipe.) A few recipes suggest sea salt or gray salt for their briny taste, or fleur de sel for its delicate flavor.

Sugar.

Pure cane sugar is preferable to beet sugar. The finer grains of baker's or superfine sugar (also labeled ultrafine, bar, castor, or caster sugar) dissolve more readily.

Powdered sugar, also called confectioners' sugar, is finely ground sugar mixed with a bit of cornstarch or tapioca starch to keep it flowing freely. It creates a sandy texture in certain cookies, and beautifully coats marshmallows.

Brown sugar gets its distinctive character from molasses. It adds golden color and rich flavor to baked goods, and tends to give cookies a chewy texture. Use light (golden) brown sugar for less color and molasses flavor, dark brown for more.

Turbinado or other coarse sugars add sparkle, and sometimes color, to cookie tops.

Sweetening syrups.

Liquid sweeteners play an important role in the texture of ice cream and other frozen desserts. In tandem with other ingredients, glucose in particular prevents ice cream from freezing rock hard and from forming coarse ice crystals. Restaurants and commercial ice cream producers often turn to glucose syrup (usually corn based) or tapioca syrup to soften ice cream without providing excess sweetness, but these are not readily available to the home cook. Both commercial and home cooks also use corn syrup. Rife with controversy—genetically modified seed, farm subsidies, industrial processing, and health concerns among them—I'd rather avoid it. Some people object to the taste, while others have allergies and sensitivities to corn products. I prefer inverted sugar syrup or other sweeteners for optimal flavor and texture.

Inverted sugar syrup sounds complicated, but really it's just table sugar (sucrose) that's been broken down into its component sugars (glucose and fructose). It's simple to make by boiling sugar with water and a bit of acid (see recipe on page 27). I found that using this syrup to replace some of the sugar in my recipes (typically about 20 percent) worked like a charm. The syrup adds no color or taste other than sweetness, letting the ice cream's own flavors shine through. (Geeky factoid: The syrup is "inverted" because the direction of polarization of light passing through it rotates the opposite way from that of light passed through a simple sugar [sucrose] syrup.)

I love **golden syrup**, a common English ingredient, for its clean, light caramel flavor. This partially inverted cane syrup, with a color and consistency similar to light honey, can be substituted 1:1 for inverted sugar syrup in the recipes in this book. Lyle's is a commonly available brand.

Agave nectar varies in its composition but is generally made up largely of fructose, which is sweeter than glucose. Choose a high-quality, light-colored agave nectar for the gentlest flavor and least impact on the ice cream's color.

Each recipe in which these syrups are used includes several options in the order of preference for that recipe, taking into consideration both flavor and color. Some recipes use **honey or maple syrup** as well.

Tapioca starch.

Ground from the cassava root, tapioca starch (also called tapioca flour) works similarly to cornstarch, but thickens to a clearer, gummier gel at a lower temperature. The thickened ice cream mixture won't coat a spoon in the same way a custard would, but will have a consistency similar to a cream sauce or thin pudding. Despite its somewhat disconcerting gelatinous consistency, the mixture turns silky smooth when spun into ice cream.

Tapioca has many advantages over egg yolks as a thickener for ice cream: no need to temper, no worry about curdling, no wasted egg whites, and easier cleanup. Tapioca is also easily accessible, dissolves readily in cold liquid, and adds little flavor. Because tapioca-thickened ice cream has less fat, its flavor is often more vibrant. Italians (particularly in the south) have long held this secret, and often thicken their gelato with starch rather than egg yolks. I use yolks only when I want eggy custard flavor, such as in the Vanilla Bean Frozen Custard for the Better-Than-It (page 41), and in the lemon curd used to flavor and thicken Lemon Curd Ice Cream (page 77).

Instant tapioca (used for tapioca pudding) can be ground into a fine powder similar to tapioca starch using a coffee or spice grinder, working with about one tablespoon at a time. Mixtures using it may take slightly longer to thicken.

Vanilla extract and beans.

Always use pure rather than imitation vanilla extract. Bourbon and Tahitian are among the most popular types, each with its own distinctive aroma and flavor profile. When using whole vanilla beans, select beans that are moist and pliable. Some recipes call for splitting a bean lengthwise, scraping the seeds into the mixture, then adding the pod as well. After removing the spent pod, rinse it well, leave it to air dry, then store in a jar of sugar to infuse it with a delicate perfume.

Yogurt, strained yogurt, labne, and crème fraîche.

These ingredients add body to ice cream, as well as a refreshing tangy note that prevents the sweetness from becoming cloying. Labne is a thick Middle-Eastern yogurt cheese with a flavor similar to sour cream. You can make something quite similar using the recipe for Strained Yogurt (page 27). Alternatively, use plain, whole-milk Greek yogurt, which is tangier, or crème fraîche (page 27), which is richer and sweeter. Each recipe in which these are used includes several options in the order of preference for that recipe.

Building Block Recipes

Inverted Sugar Syrup GF DF

MAKES ABOUT 1½ CUPS (360 ML)

Cooking sugar with water and a bit of acid breaks down sucrose into its two component sugars, glucose and fructose, which helps to produce a pleasing texture in ice cream.

2 cups (400 g) granulated sugar

1½ cups (360 ml) water

½ teaspoon cream of tartar

Stir the sugar, water, and cream of tartar in a medium-size heavy saucepan to dissolve the sugar. Heat the mixture to a boil, reduce to a simmer, cover, and cook for 5 minutes to dissolve any sugar crystals clinging to the walls of the pan. Remove the cover and simmer gently for 25 minutes longer. Set aside to cool, then pour into a clean glass jar, cover, and refrigerate for up to 2 months. (If the syrup becomes too stiff to pour, warm it by placing the bottle in a bowl of warm water for a few minutes.)

Strained Yogurt GF

MAKES ABOUT 2 CUPS (480 ML)

Similar to Middle Eastern labne (which also goes by labneh, lebneh, or lebni), this thick strained yogurt cheese adds body and a gentle tangy-fresh flavor that nicely balances the sweetness of ice cream. It's difficult to find in stores (if you can source it, try Karoun brand) but simple to make at home.

Don't hesitate to make a full recipe—use leftovers as you would use cream cheese or sour cream.

1 quart (960 ml) plain, whole milk yogurt, with no added gums, thickeners, or stabilizers

Suspend a strainer lined with several layers of cheesecloth over a bowl with space for nearly 2 cups (480 ml) of whey to collect below the strainer. (Drain off the whey as you go if it gets close to the strainer.) Empty the yogurt into the cheesecloth, fold the cheesecloth over the top to cover it, and refrigerate for 12 to 24 hours, until thick and spreadable.

Transfer the strained yogurt to an airtight container and refrigerate. Save the whey for cooking, baking, or fermenting, or discard.

Crème Fraîche GF

MAKES 1 CUP (240 ML)

Crème fraîche is a cultured cream with a sweet-tangy flavor, similar to sour cream but much more thick and dense. This simple version borrows its cultures from an already cultured milk product, so you must use one with live, active cultures. Use the freshest, best-quality cream you can find. If you have crème fraîche on hand, it will help speed development and add true crème fraîche cultures.

1 cup (240 ml) heavy cream with no emulsifiers or additives, not ultrapasteurized

2 tablespoons cultured buttermilk or plain yogurt with live active cultures

1 tablespoon crème fraîche (optional)

Pour the cream into a sparkling clean glass jar and stir in the buttermilk and the crème fraîche, if using. Cover, shake briefly, and let stand at room temperature (70°F to 75°F / 52°C to 57°C) for 24 to 36 hours, shaking the jar and checking its consistency every 8 hours or so, until the cream thickens to the consistency of a loose sour cream and tastes refreshingly tangy.

Shake the tightly covered jar one more time and refrigerate. The cream will continue to thicken and develop flavor during the first 24 hours or so of refrigeration, and should remain in good form for 10 days to 2 weeks.

Chapter 3

Classics

The first ice cream sandwiches
I remember eating were at
the pool, dropped down into the
trough of a vending machine
upon depositing a quarter.
The sandwiches in this section
capture that innocent frozen
treat of childhood, and include
remakes of other favorites,
like carrot cake, Key lime pie,
and cheesecake. There's
even one on raw cookie dough.
No guilt, just good.

Pure Nostalgia (page 30)

Pure Nostalgia

This is the quintessential sandwich: vanilla ice cream encased in a cookie that invites licking sticky chocolate crumbs from your fingers. This is the one that takes me back to Maplewood Pool in New Rochelle, New York, where I generated plenty of heat climbing the steep hill to the pool on summer afternoons, cooled down as I swam laps, and refueled with an ice cream sandwich from the vending machine before heading home for supper. The cookie is adapted, with appreciation, from a recipe by Abigail Johnson Dodge on *Fine Cooking*'s website.

Vanilla Ice Cream GF

2 cups (480 ml) whole milk

⅓ cup (67 g) granulated sugar

2 tablespoons inverted sugar syrup (page 27), golden syrup, or light agave nectar

2 tablespoons tapioca starch

¼ teaspoon kosher salt

1 cup (240 ml) heavy cream

½ teaspoon pure vanilla extract

Whisk ½ cup (120 ml) of the milk with the sugar, syrup, tapioca, and salt in a medium saucepan until no lumps remain. Stir in the remaining 1½ cups (360 ml) milk and the cream. Heat the mixture over medium-high heat, stirring with a heatproof spatula, until it begins to steam and slightly bubble at the edges. Adjust to a simmer and cook, stirring constantly, until the mixture thickens to the consistency of a cream sauce, about 3 minutes longer; do not fully boil.

Transfer the mixture to a metal bowl set over a larger bowl of ice and water. Stir occasionally until the mixture is cool, taking care not to slosh water into the bowl. Stir in the vanilla, then cover and refrigerate until very cold, at least 2 hours. Transfer the bowl to the freezer for the last half hour before spinning it.

Freeze the mixture in an ice cream maker according to the manufacturer's directions. Transfer the ice cream to a chilled container, cover, and freeze until firm but still spreadable, about 4 hours.

Soft Chocolate Cookie Bars

Neutral vegetable oil, for the parchment

1¼ cups (165 g) all-purpose flour

½ cup (50 g) unsweetened Dutch-processed cocoa powder

½ teaspoon baking soda

½ teaspoon kosher salt

6 tablespoons (85 g) unsalted butter, softened

½ cup (100 g) granulated sugar

¼ cup packed (50 g) light brown sugar

1 teaspoon pure vanilla extract

⅔ cup (160 ml) whole milk

Preheat the oven to 350°F (175°C) with a rack in the center of the oven. Line a baking sheet (preferably rimless) with parchment paper and lightly oil the parchment.

Sift the flour, cocoa powder, baking soda, and salt in a medium bowl; set aside.

Beat the butter with the granulated and brown sugar on medium-high speed using a stand mixer and the paddle attachment until light and creamy, about 3 minutes. Add the vanilla on low speed. On low speed, add half of the flour mixture, then all of the milk, then the remaining flour, scraping the bowl between additions. (Alternatively, use a handheld mixer.)

Dollop the batter all over the parchment paper, then spread it as smoothly and evenly as possible with an offset spatula to make an 18-by-12-inch (46-by-30½-cm) rectangle.

Bake just until the bar loses its shine, about 10 minutes, rotating the pan front to back halfway through baking. Remove from the oven and, while still warm, use a ruler as a guide to cut the cookie crosswise to make two 12-by-9-inch (30½-by-23-cm) cookie slabs. Use a fork to prick the surface of the slabs in neat rows, like the top of a traditional ice cream sandwich. Slide the parchment with the cookie bars onto a rack to cool completely.

SANDWICH!

Form sandwiches on a baking sheet lined with plastic wrap (rather than in a pan) using Method #4 on page 19. Once firmly frozen, cut the sandwiches into 4 strips in each direction to make 16 bars.

TAKE IT EASY

Fill store-bought chocolate cookies or thin brownies with vanilla, chocolate, coffee, strawberry, or mint chip ice cream.

DRESS IT UP

Roll the sides of the sandwiches in mini chocolate chips, toasted nuts, or toasted coconut.

Inside-Out Carrot Cake

Cream Cheese Ice Cream
on Carrot Cake Cookies

MAKES
12
SANDWICHES

I love carrot cake, except that the frosting is always too sweet and sticky. Chill it down and surround the "frosting" with cake on both sides, like a frozen carrot-cake whoopie pie, and now we're talkin'. You can use reduced-fat cream cheese (Neufchâtel) and sour cream in this recipe, but stay away from the nonfat versions.

Cream Cheese Ice Cream GF

1½ cups (360 ml) milk

½ cup (100 g) granulated sugar

2 tablespoons golden syrup, inverted sugar syrup (page 27), or agave nectar

5 teaspoons tapioca starch

½ teaspoon kosher salt

6 ounces (168 g) cream cheese, at room temperature

⅓ cup (80 ml) sour cream, at room temperature

1 teaspoon pure vanilla extract

½ teaspoon packed finely grated lemon peel

1 teaspoon fresh lemon juice

Whisk ½ cup (120 ml) of the milk with the sugar, golden syrup, tapioca, and salt in a medium saucepan until no lumps remain. Stir in the remaining 1 cup (240 ml) milk. Heat the mixture over medium-high heat, stirring with a heatproof spatula, until it begins to steam and slightly bubble at the edges. Adjust to a simmer and cook, stirring constantly, until the mixture thickens to the consistency of a cream sauce, about 2 minutes longer; do not fully boil. Set aside.

Mix the cream cheese in a bowl with a handheld electric mixer until completely smooth. Add the sour cream, vanilla, lemon peel, and lemon juice and mix until smooth. Whisk in the thickened milk just to combine. (Alternatively, use a food processor.)

Transfer the mixture to a metal bowl set over a larger bowl of ice and water. Stir occasionally until the mixture is cool, taking care not to slosh water into the bowl. Cover and refrigerate until very cold, at least 2 hours. Transfer the bowl to the freezer for the last half hour before spinning it.

Freeze the mixture in an ice cream maker according to the manufacturer's directions. When it is ready, transfer the ice cream to a chilled container. Cover and freeze until firm, at least 4 hours or overnight.

Carrot Cake Cookies DF

1 cup (132 g) all-purpose flour

⅓ cup (44 g) whole wheat pastry flour
(or additional all-purpose flour)

1 teaspoon baking powder

¼ teaspoon baking soda

¼ teaspoon ground cinnamon

½ teaspoon kosher salt

½ cup (100 g) granulated sugar

½ cup packed (100 g) light brown sugar

6 tablespoons (90 ml) neutral vegetable oil

1 large egg

1 teaspoon packed finely grated orange zest

½ teaspoon pure vanilla extract

1 cup packed (160 g) finely grated carrot

½ cup (60 g) walnuts or pecans, toasted and
coarsely chopped (see page 25)

Preheat the oven to 350°F (175°C) with racks
in the upper and lower thirds of the oven. Line
two baking sheets with parchment paper or
silicone baking mats.

Whisk together the all-purpose and whole
wheat flours, the baking powder, baking soda,
cinnamon, and salt in a small bowl. Set aside.

In a medium bowl, whisk together the
granulated and brown sugars, oil, egg, orange
zest, and vanilla. Stir in the flour mixture just to
combine. Fold in the carrots and nuts.

Scoop out tablespoons of the dough, spacing
them evenly on the prepared baking sheets
with 1 inch (2½ cm) all around each cookie, to
make 24 cookies.

Bake until the cookies are firm to the touch
and just beginning to color around the edges,
about 12 minutes, rotating the pans top to
bottom and front to back halfway through
baking. Let the cookies cool on the sheets for
5 minutes, then slide the cookies on their liners
to wire racks to cool completely.

SANDWICH!

Form sandwiches using Method #1 on page 18,
using about ⅓ cup (80 ml) of ice cream for each
sandwich.

TAKE IT EASY

Replace the cookies
with ¼-inch-thick
(6-mm) slices of
unfrosted carrot cake,
or cut carrot cake
muffins into
crosswise slices.

DRESS IT UP

Roll the sides of
the sandwiches in
chopped toasted nuts
or shredded coconut.

Key Lime Pie

Key Lime Ice Cream
on Sugar Cookies

MAKES
12
SANDWICHES

These sandwiches enclose familiar sweet-tart Key lime filling—made into a rich, creamy ice cream—between cookies that shatter like flaky pie crust. A handheld, bar-style citrus squeezer eases the work of juicing the small limes. If diminutive, pale, super-juicy Key limes aren't available in your area, substitute common (Persian) limes or bottled 100% Key lime juice. The cookie dough is easy to work with, forgiving (any tears may be easily patched), and holds its shape when baked, perfect for cutting shapes with cookie cutters or molds. Note that larger molds or cutters will yield fewer sandwiches.

Key Lime Ice Cream GF

1½ cups (360 ml) whole milk

1 cup (200 g) granulated sugar

3 tablespoons golden syrup, inverted sugar syrup (page 27), or light agave nectar

2 tablespoons tapioca starch

¼ teaspoon kosher salt

1 cup (240 ml) heavy cream, at room temperature

2 tablespoons strained yogurt (page 27), labne, or plain Greek yogurt, at room temperature

½ cup (120 ml) Key lime juice (about 14 limes), at room temperature

1 teaspoon packed finely grated zest from Key limes or common limes

Whisk ½ cup (120 ml) of the milk with the sugar, golden syrup, tapioca, and salt in a medium saucepan until no lumps remain. Whisk in the remaining 1 cup (240 ml) milk.

Heat the mixture over medium-high heat, stirring with a heatproof spatula, until it begins to steam and slightly bubble at the edges. Adjust to a simmer and cook, stirring constantly, until the mixture thickens to the consistency of a cream sauce, about 90 seconds longer; do not fully boil. Remove from the heat.

Whisk the cream and yogurt in a medium bowl until smooth. Whisk in the lime juice and zest. Stir in the thickened milk mixture. (Don't worry if the mixture appears curdled.)

Cover and refrigerate until very cold, at least 2 hours. Transfer the bowl to the freezer for the last half hour before spinning it.

Strain the mixture through a fine-mesh

strainer to remove the zest, then freeze in an ice cream maker according to the manufacturer's directions.

While the ice cream spins, line a 13-by-9-inch (33-by-23-cm) baking pan with waxed paper so that it extends beyond the pan on two sides. Place the pan in the freezer. When the ice cream is ready, spread it evenly in the pan and cover with plastic wrap, pressing it directly against the ice cream. Freeze until firm, 4 to 6 hours.

Sugar Cookies

1½ cups (200 g) all-purpose flour

⅓ cup (40 g) powdered sugar

½ teaspoon packed finely grated Key lime zest

½ teaspoon kosher salt

½ cup (1 stick /113 g) unsalted butter, softened

2 tablespoons milk

½ teaspoon pure vanilla extract

2 tablespoons turbinado or other coarse sugar, for sprinkling

Preheat the oven to 350°F (175°C) with racks in the upper and lower thirds of the oven. Line two baking sheets with parchment paper or silicone baking mats.

Pulse the flour, sugar, lime zest, and salt in a food processor. Add the butter and process until the mixture has the appearance of wet sand. Add the milk and vanilla and process until the dough forms a ball. (Alternatively, cream the butter and sugar in a bowl and add the dry ingredients until thoroughly combined.)

Transfer the dough to a sheet of parchment paper on a flat surface, cover with plastic wrap, and use a pin to roll it to ⅛ inch (3 mm) thick. Use a 2½-inch (6-cm) cutter or ice cream sandwich molds to cut approximately 24 cookies (depending on size and shape of cutter) from the dough, gathering up and re-rolling the dough one to two times more, if needed, to make all the cookies. Transfer the cookies to the prepared sheets, spacing them evenly. Sprinkle the tops with turbinado sugar.

Bake until the cookies are just beginning to color at the edges, 11 to 13 minutes, rotating the pans top to bottom and front to back halfway through baking. Let the cookies cool on the pans for 5 minutes, then transfer them on their liners to wire racks to cool completely.

SANDWICH!

Form sandwiches using Method #3 on page 19, using the same cutter used for the cookies to cut out 12 shapes, or half as many ice cream shapes as you have cookies, gathering scraps to form the last few, if needed. Alternatively, form the sandwiches using ice cream sandwich molds following Method #2.

TAKE IT EASY
Use store-bought sugar cookies or other cookies. Stir Key lime juice or prepared limeade into softened vanilla ice cream.

DRESS IT UP
Roll the sides of the sandwiches in graham cracker crumbs.

Key Lime Pie (bottom left, page 35) and New York Cheesecake (bottom right, page 38)

New York Cheesecake

Cherry Cheesecake Ice Cream on Shortcrust Cookies

MAKES **12** SANDWICHES

Close your eyes, picture yourself at a booth in your favorite New York diner, and you just might believe this sandwich is an icy-cold slice of cheesecake. Smooth, sweet, and creamy, with a touch of lemon, it's an iconic taste. You can argue 'til the cows come home about Junior's versus Lindy's, graham cracker versus shortcrust, sour cream topping or not. One thing you won't have to worry about: the top of your cheesecake cracking in the oven.

You can use reduced-fat cream cheese (Neufchâtel) and sour cream in this recipe, but stay away from the nonfat versions. For strawberry cheesecake ice cream, substitute strawberries for the cherries in the Cherry Swirl mix-in.

Cherry Cheesecake Ice Cream GF

1 ¼ cups (300 ml) milk

½ cup (100 g) granulated sugar

2 tablespoons inverted sugar syrup (page 27), golden syrup, or light agave nectar

1 tablespoon tapioca starch

½ teaspoon kosher salt

6 ounces (168 g) cream cheese, at room temperature

⅓ cup (80 ml) sour cream, at room temperature

1 teaspoon pure vanilla extract

1 teaspoon packed finely grated lemon zest

1 teaspoon fresh lemon juice

1 recipe Cherry Swirl (page 160)

Whisk ½ cup (120 ml) of the milk with the sugar, syrup, tapioca, and salt in a medium saucepan until no lumps remain. Stir in the remaining ¾ cup (180 ml) milk. Heat the mixture over medium-high heat, stirring with a heatproof spatula, until it begins to steam and slightly bubble at the edges. Adjust to a simmer and cook, stirring constantly, until the mixture thickens to the consistency of a cream sauce, about 90 seconds longer; do not fully boil. Set aside.

Mix the cream cheese in a bowl with a handheld electric mixer until completely smooth. Add the sour cream, vanilla, lemon zest, and lemon juice and mix until smooth. Briefly mix in the thickened milk, just enough to combine everything evenly. (Alternatively, use a food processor.)

Transfer the mixture to a metal bowl set over a larger bowl of ice and water. Stir occasionally until the mixture is cool, taking care not to slosh water into the bowl. Cover and refrigerate until very cold, at least 2 hours. Transfer the bowl to the freezer for the last half hour before spinning it.

Freeze the mixture in an ice cream maker according to the manufacturer's directions. When it is ready, transfer the ice cream to a chilled container, adding in the swirl as you go (see page 156). Cover and freeze until firm, at least 6 hours or overnight.

Shortcrust Cookies

1 cup (132 g) all-purpose flour

1 teaspoon baking powder

½ teaspoon kosher salt

½ cup (1 stick /113 g) unsalted butter, softened

¾ cup (150 g) granulated sugar

½ teaspoon finely grated lemon zest

½ teaspoon pure vanilla extract

2 tablespoons turbinado or coarse sugar, for sprinkling

Preheat the oven to 325°F (165°C) with racks in the upper and lower thirds of the oven. Line two baking sheets with parchment paper or silicone baking mats.

Whisk together the flour, baking powder, and salt in a small bowl. Set aside.

Beat the butter and sugar in a medium bowl with a handheld electric mixer until creamy. (Alternatively, use a wooden spoon.) Add the lemon zest and vanilla. Mix in the flour mixture just until well combined. (If using a mixer, it may be easier to finish the mixing by hand.)

Divide the dough into 24 pieces, rolling each between your palms into a smooth ball. Dunk one side of each ball in turbinado sugar and space them evenly on the baking sheets, sugar-side up. Use a flat-bottom drinking glass to flatten each ball to ¼-inch (6-mm) thickness. (Moisten the glass bottom or spray it with nonstick pan spray if the dough sticks.)

Bake until the cookies are light golden around the edges, 12 to 14 minutes, rotating the pans top to bottom and front to back halfway through baking. Let the cookies cool on the sheets for 5 minutes, then slide the cookies on their liners to wire racks to cool completely.

SANDWICH!

Form sandwiches using Method #1 on page 18.

TAKE IT EASY
Substitute store-bought sugar or butter cookies.

DRESS IT UP
Roll the sides of the sandwiches in chopped dried cherries.

Better-Than-It

MAKES **12** SANDWICHES

The It's-It company began selling scoops of vanilla ice cream sandwiched between old-fashioned oatmeal cookies cloaked in chocolate at San Francisco's Playland at the Beach in 1928. By the time I moved to the area in 1978, the It's-It was a well established local phenomenon. I've filled my version of the novelty with a not-overly-sweet vanilla frozen custard.

Don't be put off by the recipe's many steps: Each is reasonably quick and easy, and one bite will convince you it was all worthwhile. I half-dip the sandwiches for a pretty finish. If you wish to fully dip them, double the Chocolate Shell recipe.

Vanilla Bean Frozen Custard GF

4 large egg yolks

1 tablespoon plus ⅓ cup (79 g) granulated sugar

1½ cups (360 ml) milk, whole or 2%

3 tablespoons golden syrup, inverted sugar syrup (page 27) or light agave nectar

1 tablespoon tapioca starch

¼ teaspoon kosher salt

2 cups (480 ml) heavy cream

1 vanilla bean, split lengthwise

1 teaspoon pure vanilla extract

Whisk the yolks with 1 tablespoon of the sugar in a medium bowl until smooth and slightly thickened. Set aside.

Whisk ½ cup (120 ml) of the milk with the syrup, tapioca, salt, and the remaining ⅓ cup (67 g) sugar in a medium saucepan until no lumps remain. Stir in the cream and the remaining 1 cup (240 ml) milk. Use a paring knife to scrape in the seeds from the vanilla bean; toss in the pod. Heat the mixture over medium-high heat, stirring with a heatproof spatula, until it begins to steam and slightly bubble at the edges.

Ladle 1 cup (240 ml) of the hot mixture into the yolks in a stream as you whisk the mixture to prevent the yolks from scrambling. Whisk the mixture back into the saucepan and cook at a slow simmer, stirring with a spatula, until the mixture thickens enough to thickly coat a spoon, 1 to 2 minutes longer.

Strain the mixture through a fine-mesh strainer into a metal bowl. (Rinse and save the pod for another use, page 26, or discard.) Stir in the vanilla extract.

Set the bowl over a larger bowl of ice and water. Stir occasionally until the mixture is cool, taking care not to slosh water into the bowl. Cover and refrigerate until very cold, at least 2 hours. Transfer the bowl to the freezer for the last half hour before spinning it.

Freeze the mixture in an ice cream maker according to the manufacturer's directions. When it is ready, transfer the ice cream to a chilled container. Cover and freeze until firm, at least 4 hours or overnight.

Oatmeal Cookies GF OPTION

¾ cup (100 g) white whole wheat, whole wheat, or oat flour

½ teaspoon baking soda

½ teaspoon baking powder

½ teaspoon kosher salt

½ cup (1 stick / 113 g) unsalted butter, softened

⅔ cup packed (134 g) light brown sugar

1 large egg

½ teaspoon pure vanilla extract

1½ cups (180 g) rolled oats

½ cup (80 g) raisins (optional)

Preheat the oven to 350°F (175°C) with racks in the upper and lower thirds of the oven. Line two baking sheets with parchment paper or silicone baking mats. Whisk together the flour, baking soda, baking powder, and salt in a small bowl.

Put the butter and brown sugar in a mixing bowl and use a wooden spoon or a handheld electric mixer to mix until they are creamy. Add the egg and vanilla and mix until smooth. Stir in the flour mixture just until everything is well combined, then stir in the oats and raisins, if using.

Spoon or scoop the batter in tablespoons onto the prepared baking sheets, spacing them evenly, to make 24 cookies. Press the cookies with lightly dampened fingers to flatten them slightly—they will spread further as they bake. Bake until the cookies are light golden around the edges, 8 to 10 minutes, rotating the pans top to bottom and front to back halfway through baking.

Let the cookies cool on the pan for 5 minutes, then transfer them directly to a wire rack to cool completely, sliding a spatula under them if they do not release easily.

Chocolate Shell

1 recipe Chocolate Shell (page 165), made with extra bittersweet (64 to 72 percent) chocolate

SANDWICH!

Form sandwiches using Method #1 on page 18 and freeze until firm, at least 2 hours, before dipping. Dip the sandwiches to coat them halfway in chocolate following the instructions for Chocolate Shell on page 165.

TAKE IT EASY

Use store-bought oatmeal cookies and vanilla ice cream.

DRESS IT UP

Immediately after dipping each sandwich, dunk the soft chocolate into a bowl of chopped toasted nuts.

Wake-up Call

Espresso Caramel Swirl
Ice Cream on Espresso
Fudge Brownies

MAKES
16
SANDWICHES

In need of an early morning wake-up or an afternoon pick-me-up but no Red Bull in sight? This candy bar of a sandwich is sweet, sticky, and packed with caffeine from both chocolate and espresso. There's plenty of coffee flavor for even the most demanding, triple-shot aficionado, with espresso threaded through the ice cream and echoed in the brownie. Power on! (For a lower-volt jolt, use decaf espresso.)

Espresso Caramel Swirl Ice Cream GF

1½ cups (360 ml) whole milk

⅓ cup (67 g) granulated sugar

2 tablespoons golden syrup, inverted sugar syrup (page 27), or agave nectar

2 tablespoons tapioca starch

¼ teaspoon kosher salt

1 cup (240 ml) heavy cream

½ teaspoon vanilla extract

½ cup (120 ml) Espresso Caramel Swirl (page 158)

Whisk ½ cup (120 ml) of the milk with the sugar, golden syrup, tapioca, and salt in a medium saucepan until no lumps remain. Stir in the remaining 1 cup (240 ml) milk and the cream. Heat the mixture over medium-high heat, stirring with a heatproof spatula, until it begins to steam and slightly bubble at the edges. Adjust to a simmer and cook, stirring constantly, until the mixture thickens to the consistency of a cream sauce, 2 to 3 minutes longer; do not fully boil.

Transfer the mixture to a metal bowl set over a larger bowl of ice and water. Stir occasionally until the mixture is cool, taking care not to slosh water into the bowl. Stir in the vanilla, then cover and refrigerate until very cold, at least 2 hours. Transfer the bowl to the freezer for the last half hour before spinning it.

Freeze the mixture in an ice cream maker according to the manufacturer's directions. When it is ready, transfer the ice cream to a chilled container, layering it with the Espresso Caramel Swirl as you pack the ice cream into the container (see page 156). Cover and freeze until firm but spreadable, about 6 hours.

(continued on page 46)

Espresso Fudge Brownies

Neutral vegetable oil, for the parchment

6 ounces (170 g) chopped bittersweet (60 to 65 percent) chocolate

½ cup (1 stick / 113 g) unsalted butter

⅔ cup (134 g) granulated sugar

1 teaspoon instant espresso granules

1 teaspoon pure vanilla extract

¼ teaspoon kosher salt

2 large eggs, at room temperature

1 cup (132 g) all-purpose flour

½ teaspoon baking powder

Preheat the oven to 350°F (175°C) with racks in the upper and lower thirds of the oven. Line two 8-inch (20-cm) square pans with lightly oiled parchment paper or foil to cover the bottom and run up two sides to the top of the pan as a sling to later aid in lifting the brownies from the pans. (Alternatively, bake the brownies in a 13-by-9-inch / 33-by-23-cm pan.)

Melt the chocolate and butter in a medium metal bowl nested over a saucepan holding about 1 inch (2½ cm) of simmering water. Remove the bowl from the heat and wipe the bottom dry.

Whisk the sugar, espresso, vanilla, and salt into the melted chocolate. Whisk in the eggs one at a time, mixing each until smooth. Stir the baking powder into the flour, then stir the mixture into the batter with a spatula just until no white streaks remain.

Divide the batter equally between the pans, spreading each into an even layer, smoothing the tops with a spatula. Bake until the tops feel firm but a toothpick inserted near the center finds some moist crumbs clinging to it, about 15 minutes, rotating the pans top to bottom and front to back halfway through baking. Let the brownie layers cool in the pans for 10 minutes, then lift out the brownies using the parchment slings and transfer them on the parchment to wire racks to cool completely.

Refrigerate the brownie layers until cold and firm, 1 to 2 hours.

SANDWICH!

Form sandwiches using Method #4 on page 19. Once firmly frozen, cut the sandwiches into 4 strips in each direction to form 16 bars.

TAKE IT EASY

Use a brownie mix, adding 1 teaspoon of instant espresso granules and baking the brownies in two pans until still slightly moist at the center, about 5 minutes less than specified on the box. Swirl the Espresso Caramel Swirl into softened vanilla ice cream, or swirl store-bought cara-mel into softened coffee ice cream.

DRESS IT UP

Roll the sides in chopped chocolate-covered espresso beans. Or dip the ends of the brownie bars into Chocolate Shell (page 165).

Bella Nutella

Chocolate-Hazelnut Ice Cream
on Hazelnut Sandies

MAKES 10 SANDWICHES

While I was assisting Rosetta Costantino with her forthcoming book *Southern Italian Desserts*, her son Adrian worked out a beautifully smooth and flavorful chocolate-hazelnut paste that trumped anything we could find in a jar. I've adapted his formula and spun it right into the ice cream. The buttery cookies echo the ice cream's dark-roasted hazelnut flavor.

Chocolate-Hazelnut Ice Cream GF

1½ cups (360 ml) whole milk

⅔ cup (134 g) granulated sugar

2 tablespoons golden syrup, inverted sugar syrup (page 27), or agave nectar

5 teaspoons tapioca starch

¼ teaspoon kosher salt

⅓ cup (67 g) chopped bittersweet (60 to 70 percent) chocolate

½ cup (188 g) Chocolate-Hazelnut Spread (page 160)

1 cup (240 ml) heavy cream

Chopped toasted hazelnuts or finely chopped chocolate, for mix-ins (optional)

Whisk ½ cup (120 ml) of the milk with the sugar, golden syrup, tapioca, and salt in a medium saucepan until no lumps remain. Stir in the remaining 1 cup (240 ml) milk. Heat the mixture over medium-high heat, stirring with a heatproof spatula, until it begins to steam and slightly bubble at the edges. Adjust to a simmer and cook, stirring constantly, until the mixture thickens to the consistency of a cream sauce, about 90 seconds longer; do not fully boil. Remove from the heat, drop the chopped chocolate and chocolate-hazelnut paste into the pan without stirring, cover, and let stand for 2 minutes to melt the chocolate. Stir the mixture until smooth.

Transfer the mixture to a metal bowl. Stir in the cream until well combined. Set the bowl over a larger bowl of ice and water. Stir occasionally until the mixture is cool, taking care not to slosh water into the bowl. Cover and refrigerate until very cold, at least 2 hours. Transfer the bowl to the freezer for the last half hour before spinning it.

Freeze the mixture in an ice cream maker according to the manufacturer's directions. If you are using them, add the chopped hazelnuts or chocolate at the end of processing.

While the ice cream spins, line a 9-inch (23-cm) square baking pan with waxed paper and place it in the freezer. When the ice cream is ready, spread it evenly into the prepared pan, cover with plastic wrap, pressing it directly against the surface, and freeze until firm, at least 4 hours.

Hazelnut Sandies

½ cup (70 g) hazelnuts, toasted and skinned (see page 25)

½ cup (1 stick / 113 g) unsalted butter, softened

⅓ cup (40 g) powdered sugar

1 cup (132 g) all-purpose flour

¼ teaspoon kosher salt

2 tablespoons turbinado or other coarse sugar

Pulse the nuts in a food processor to coarsely chop them. Add the butter and powdered sugar and process until smooth and creamy, about 1 minute, stopping to scrape down the bowl as needed. Add the flour and salt, pulsing several times until the dough is well blended. The dough should hold together when you press it between your fingers.

Transfer the dough to a lightly floured surface and bring it together into a mass, then shape it into a 5¼-inch (13-cm) log with flat (not tapered) ends.

Lay a sheet of plastic wrap on a flat surface and sprinkle it with the turbinado sugar. Roll the log across the sugar, pressing it into the sugar to coat it evenly. Wrap the log tightly in the plastic, press the ends against a flat surface to flatten them, and refrigerate until very firm, about 2 hours, or freeze for 30 minutes.

About 20 minutes before baking, preheat the oven to 350°F (175°C) with racks in the upper and lower thirds of the oven. Line two baking sheets with parchment paper or silicone baking mats.

Unwrap the log and use a thin, sharp knife to shave ⅛ inch (3 mm) off of each end (press together into a cookie and bake as a snack), then cut the log into twenty ¼-inch-thick (6-mm) slices. Evenly space the cookies on the prepared baking sheets and bake until the cookies begin to color around the edges, 13 to 15 minutes, rotating the pans top to bottom and front to back halfway through baking. Let the cookies cool on the pans for 5 minutes, then slide the cookies on their liners to a wire rack to cool completely.

SANDWICH!

Form sandwiches using Method #3 on page 19, using a 2½-inch (6-cm) cutter to cut out 10 rounds of the ice cream, gathering scraps to form the last round or two, if needed. Alternatively, form sandwiches using Method #1.

TAKE IT EASY

Use store-bought hazelnut or chocolate cookies in place of the sandies. Swirl store-bought chocolate-hazelnut paste or chopped toasted hazelnuts into softened chocolate ice cream.

DRESS IT UP

Smear more chocolate-hazelnut spread on one cookie in each pair before sandwiching, or roll the sides in chopped toasted hazelnuts or mini chocolate chips.

Good 'n' Nutty

Toasted Almond Ice Cream
on Almond Wafers

MAKES
12
SANDWICHES

Crispy, rustic-shaped almond wafers stuffed with nut-textured ice cream pack a one-two almond punch in this nut lover's sandwich. For a completely smooth ice cream, strain out the almonds right before spinning, which will slightly reduce the yield. For perfectly round cookies, immediately after removing them from the oven, use a 2½- to 3-inch (5- to 7½-cm) round cutter to cut the cookies into rounds.

Toasted Almond Ice Cream GF

⅔ cup (100 g) blanched almonds, toasted and completely cooled (see page 25)

½ cup (100 g) granulated sugar

1½ cups (360 ml) whole milk

2 tablespoons tapioca starch

2 tablespoons mild-flavored honey, golden syrup, or inverted sugar syrup (page 27)

¼ teaspoon kosher salt

1½ cups (360 ml) heavy cream

½ teaspoon pure vanilla extract

Process the nuts in a food processor with the sugar until they are almost the texture of flour, occasionally scraping down the bowl and taking care not to overprocess them into almond butter. Set aside.

Whisk ½ cup (120 ml) of the milk with the tapioca, honey, and salt in a medium saucepan until no lumps remain. Stir in the remaining 1 cup (240 ml) milk and the cream. Heat the mixture over medium-high heat, stirring with a heatproof spatula, until it begins to steam and slightly bubble at the edges. Adjust to a simmer and cook, stirring constantly, until the mixture thickens to the consistency of a cream sauce, about 2 minutes longer; do not fully boil.

Transfer the mixture to a metal bowl and stir in the almonds and vanilla. Set the bowl over a larger bowl of ice and water and stir occasionally until the mixture is cool, taking care not to slosh water into the bowl. Cover and refrigerate until very cold, at least 2 hours. Transfer the bowl to the freezer for the last half hour before spinning it.

Freeze the mixture in an ice cream maker according to the manufacturer's directions. When it is ready, transfer the ice cream to a chilled container, cover, and freeze until firm, at least 4 hours or overnight.

Almond Wafers

⅓ cup (44 g) all-purpose flour

½ cup (100 g) granulated sugar

¼ teaspoon kosher salt

3 large egg whites

¼ cup (½ stick / 56 g) unsalted butter, melted and cooled, plus more for the pans

1 cup (130 g) sliced almonds

Whisk the flour, sugar, and salt in a small bowl. Stir in the egg whites, then the melted butter, until well mixed. Stir in the almonds to evenly coat them. Refrigerate the batter for 30 minutes.

Preheat the oven to 350°F (175°C) with racks in the upper and lower thirds of the oven. Line two rimless baking sheets with parchment paper. Lightly rub or brush butter over the parchment paper.

Drop the batter in heaping teaspoons to form 12 mounds on each pan, making 24 in total, with plenty of space all around each. Use a small offset spatula or the back of a spoon to spread the batter into neat 2½-inch (6-cm) rounds about as thick as a single almond slice (lightly spray the spatula with pan spray if the dough sticks), leaving ½ inch (1½ cm) all around each cookie for spreading.

Bake until most of each cookie's surface is golden, 15 to 18 minutes, rotating the pans top to bottom and front to back halfway through baking. Immediately slide the cookies on their liners to a flat surface and use a paring knife to quickly trim any that have flowed together, then transfer the cookies on their liners to wire racks to cool completely.

SANDWICH!

Form sandwiches using Method #1 on page 18, using ¼ to ⅓ cup (60 to 80 ml) of ice cream per sandwich. Take care as you sandwich them, pressing gently to avoid shattering the delicate wafers. These sandwiches are best enjoyed up to 48 hours after filling them. For longer storage, freeze the ice cream and cookies separately and form the sandwiches shortly before serving them.

TAKE IT EASY

Use store-bought almond cookies and toasted almond ice cream.

DRESS IT UP

Roll the sides of the sandwiches in Almond Crack (page 163) or chopped chocolate-covered almonds. Or paint Chocolate Shell (page 165) on the cookie bottoms before sandwiching.

Cookie Monster

Chocolate Chip Ice Cream
on Cookie Dough

MAKES
16
SANDWICHES

Yep, you read that right—an ice cream sandwich built right on the cookie dough, no baking required. The suggestion came from my partner in sandwiches, Laura Werlin, who mines the savory side of sandwiches in her books *Great Grilled Cheese* and *Grilled Cheese Please!*

The cookie dough is made without eggs, so there's no need to fear eating it raw. It's firm enough to stand up to the ice cream, yet chewy when frozen. Thanks, Laura—why didn't *I* think of that?

The chocolate chip ice cream is made *stracciatella* style: As melted chocolate is drizzled into the spinning ice cream machine, it hardens into "shreds" that melt smoothly on your tongue. This sandwich is perfect for cutting into bite-size treats for a party or potluck.

Chocolate Chip Ice Cream GF

2 cups (480 ml) whole milk

⅓ cup (67 g) granulated sugar

2 tablespoons golden syrup, inverted sugar syrup (page 27) or light agave nectar

2 tablespoons tapioca starch

¼ teaspoon kosher salt

1 cup (240 ml) heavy cream

½ teaspoon pure vanilla extract

½ cup (100 g) bittersweet (60 to 70 percent) chocolate, chopped or chips

1 tablespoon neutral vegetable oil or coconut oil

Whisk ½ cup (120 ml) of the milk with the sugar, syrup, tapioca, and salt in a medium saucepan until no lumps remain. Stir in the remaining 1½ cups (360 ml) milk and the cream. Heat the mixture over medium-high heat, stirring with a heatproof spatula, until it begins to steam and slightly bubble at the edges. Adjust to a simmer and cook, stirring constantly, until the mixture thickens to the consistency of a cream sauce, about 3 minutes longer; do not fully boil.

Transfer the mixture to a metal bowl set over a larger bowl of ice and water. Stir occasionally until the mixture is cool, taking care not to slosh water into the bowl. Stir in the vanilla, then cover and refrigerate until very cold, at least 2 hours.

Transfer the bowl to the freezer for the last half hour before spinning it.

Freeze the mixture in an ice cream maker according to the manufacturer's directions. While the mixture spins, melt the chocolate and oil in the microwave or in a small saucepan until you can stir it smooth. Let cool to room temperature, keeping it fluid.

With the machine running, drizzle in the cooled melted chocolate during the last minute of spinning. (Alternatively, drizzle the chocolate over the ice cream as you transfer it to the container, folding it in with a spatula or ice cream paddle to break it up as you go.) Transfer the ice cream to a chilled container, cover, and freeze until firm but still spreadable, at least 4 hours.

Cookie Dough

½ cup (1 stick / 113 g) unsalted butter

⅓ cup packed (67 g) light brown sugar

¼ cup (50 g) granulated sugar

2 tablespoons milk, whole or 2%

½ teaspoon pure vanilla extract

½ teaspoon kosher salt

1¼ cup (165 g) all-purpose flour

1 cup (200 g) mini chocolate chips

Neutral vegetable oil, for the waxed or parchment paper

Melt the butter with the brown and granulated sugar in a small saucepan, stirring to dissolve the sugar. Transfer to a bowl and stir in the milk, vanilla, and salt until well blended. Stir in the flour until completely smooth. Let cool completely, then stir in the chips. (If the chips begin to melt, stop stirring—the swirls will be pretty.)

Line an 8-inch (20-cm) square freezer-safe baking pan with two pieces of lightly oiled waxed paper or parchment paper so that the papers extend well beyond the edges of the pan on all four sides as a sling for easy removal. Scatter

half of the dough into the pan and use your fingers to pack it into an even layer. Top with lightly oiled waxed or parchment paper, oiled side down.

Place another lightly oiled waxed or parchment paper in the pan, leaving 2 inches (5 cm) of paper extending at each end. Scatter and press the remaining dough into an even layer. Top with lightly oiled waxed paper or parchment, oiled side down. Freeze the dough layers until firm, at least 1 hour.

SANDWICH!

Use the flaps to lift out the top cookie dough layer. Peel the paper from one side and loosely replace it. Flip the layer over and do the same to the other side. Repeat with the second cookie dough layer. Place both layers back in the freezer.

Form sandwiches using Method #4 on page 19, starting with step 3, using the bottom two pieces of parchment extended on all sides to line the pan in place of the plastic wrap. Freeze hard before cutting the sandwiches into 4 strips in each direction to form 16 bars. To make 64 bite-size treats, cut each bar into quarters.

TAKE IT EASY

Substitute store-bought chocolate chip or fudge ripple ice cream.

DRESS IT UP

Add ½ cup (60 g) chopped walnuts to the cookie dough, or roll the edges of the sandwiches in lightly toasted chopped walnuts.

Chapter

4

Farm Fresh

Nothing says summer like the season's freshest fruits churned into a bucket of ice cream. But why ignore the other three seasons? These sandwiches work their way through the whole year's bounty, from early spring strawberries to summer peaches to winter citrus—plus a tropical treat and a honey and goat's milk sandwich to enjoy anytime.

Rhubarb Crumble (top left and with granola, page 60) and Strawberry Patch (top right, page 58)

Strawberry Patch

Strawberry-Balsamic Frozen Yogurt on Black Pepper Cookies

MAKES **12** SANDWICHES

Have you ever drizzled balsamic vinegar over your strawberries, then sprinkled them with black pepper? This sandwich recreates that intoxicating combination, which coaxes the best from even imperfect berries. The "fudge" isn't actually made with chocolate, but rather by cooking balsamic vinegar down to a rich, fudge-textured syrup.

My friend Thy Tran (wanderingspoon.com), the founder and director of the Asian Culinary Forum, brought these subtly spiced pepper cookies to a holiday cookie exchange at my home several years ago. Thankfully, she also brought the recipe printed from an article in *Sunset Magazine*, which I've adapted here.

Strawberry-Balsamic Frozen Yogurt GF

1 pound (454 g) fresh strawberries, hulled and sliced

⅔ cup (134 g) granulated sugar

¼ teaspoon kosher salt

1¼ cups (300 ml) heavy cream

2 tablespoons mild-flavored honey, golden syrup, or inverted sugar syrup (page 27)

1 tablespoon tapioca starch

1 cup (227 g) plain Greek yogurt or strained yogurt (page 27), whole or 2%, at room temperature

1 recipe Balsamic "Fudge" Ripple (page 158)

Stir the strawberries, sugar, and salt in a bowl. Set aside for 1 hour to get juicy.

While the strawberries sit, stir ½ cup (120 ml) of the cream with the honey and tapioca in a medium saucepan until no lumps remain. Stir in the remaining ¾ cup (180 ml) cream. Heat the mixture over medium-high heat, stirring with a heatproof spatula, until it begins to steam and slightly bubble at the edges. Adjust to a simmer and cook, stirring constantly, until the mixture thickens to the consistency of a cream sauce, about 1 minute longer; do not fully boil.

Transfer the mixture to a medium bowl and set aside to cool. Set a strainer over the bowl of thickened cream.

Process the strawberries and all of their juices in a blender or food processor until the mixture is smooth. Strain the strawberries into the cream, stirring and pressing on the remaining solids to extract as much juice and pulp as possible; discard the remaining solids. Whisk the yogurt briefly to smooth it, then whisk it into the strawberry mixture.

Cover and refrigerate until very cold, at least 2 hours. Transfer the bowl to the freezer for the last half hour before spinning it.

Freeze the mixture in an ice cream maker according to the manufacturer's directions. When it is ready, transfer the ice cream to a chilled container, swirling it with the Balsamic "Fudge" as you pack the ice cream into the container (see page 156). Cover and freeze until firm, at least 6 hours or overnight.

Black Pepper Cookies

1 teaspoon black peppercorns

1 cup (132 g) all-purpose flour

1 teaspoon baking powder

¼ teaspoon kosher salt

½ cup (1 stick / 113 g) unsalted butter, softened

¾ cup (150 g) granulated sugar

2 tablespoons coarse sugar or granulated sugar, for sprinkling

Preheat the oven to 300°F (150°C) with racks in the upper and lower thirds of the oven. Line two baking sheets with parchment paper or silicone baking mats.

Crush the peppercorns: Place them on a flat surface in a plastic or paper bag and press a cast-iron skillet or other heavy pan over them, rocking and twisting it to coarsely grind the peppercorns.

Whisk together the flour, baking powder, salt, and crushed peppercorns in a small bowl. Set aside.

Beat the butter and sugar in a medium bowl with a handheld electric mixer until creamy. (Alternatively, use a wooden spoon.) Mix in the flour mixture just until well combined. (If using

a mixer, it may be easier to finish the mixing by hand.)

Divide the dough into 24 pieces, rolling each between your palms into a smooth ball. Dunk one side of each ball in coarse sugar and space them evenly on the baking sheets, sugar-side up. Use a flat-bottom drinking glass to flatten each ball to a 2½-inch (6-cm) round. (Moisten the glass bottom or spray it with nonstick pan spray if the dough sticks.)

Bake until the cookies are light golden around the edges, about 17 minutes, rotating the pans top to bottom and front to back halfway through baking.

Let the cookies cool on the sheets for 5 minutes, then slide the cookies on their liners to wire racks to cool completely.

SANDWICH!

Form sandwiches using Method #1 on page 18.

TAKE IT EASY

Use store-bought shortbread cookies and add a few twists of freshly ground black pepper to the ice cream instead. Swirl Balsamic "Fudge" into softened strawberry ice cream, or drizzle the ice cream with aged balsamic.

DRESS IT UP

Roll the sandwich sides in freeze-dried strawberry slices just before serving.

Rhubarb Crumble

Rhubarb Ice Cream on Brown Sugar Oat Cakes

MAKES 12 SANDWICHES

Rhubarb opens the spring produce season, when the garden awakens from its long winter's nap, bringing forth fruits perfect for cobblers and crisps. Botanically a vegetable but most commonly prepared as a dessert, rhubarb varieties range from green to pink or crimson, with field varieties found at farmers' markets often having the best flavor. Look for firm, crisp, bright red stalks, and discard the leaves, which are toxic.

Baby oats, also known as quick oats, are rolled oats cut into small flakes. Make your own by pulsing rolled oats in a blender or food processor until they are in small flecks. Instant oatmeal is not right for this recipe.

Rhubarb Ice Cream GF

1½ pounds (680 g) trimmed rhubarb stalks, cut into ½-inch (1½-cm) dice (about 8 stalks)

¾ cup (150 g) granulated sugar

2 teaspoons fresh lime juice

1 cup (240 ml) whole milk

2 tablespoons golden syrup, mild-flavored honey, or inverted sugar syrup (page 27)

2 tablespoons tapioca starch

¼ teaspoon kosher salt

1 cup (240 ml) heavy cream

½ teaspoon pure vanilla extract

Stir the rhubarb, sugar, and 2 tablespoons of water in a large, heavy, nonreactive saucepan over medium heat until the liquid boils. Reduce the heat to a slow simmer and cook until the fruit falls apart completely, about 10 minutes. Remove from the heat and stir in the lime juice. Set aside.

Whisk together ½ cup (120 ml) of the milk with the golden syrup, tapioca, and salt in a medium saucepan until no lumps remain. Stir in the remaining ½ cup (120 ml) milk and the cream. Heat the mixture over medium-high heat, stirring with a heatproof spatula, until it begins to steam and slightly bubble at the edges. Adjust to a simmer and cook, stirring constantly, until the mixture thickens to the consistency of a cream sauce, 2 to 3 minutes longer; do not fully boil. Remove from the heat and stir in the vanilla and the cooked rhubarb.

Transfer the mixture to a metal bowl set over a larger bowl of ice and water. Stir occasionally until the mixture is cool, taking care not to slosh water into the bowl. Cover and refrigerate until very cold, at least 2 hours. Transfer the bowl to the freezer for the last half hour before spinning it.

Freeze the mixture in an ice cream maker according to the manufacturer's directions. When it is ready, transfer the ice cream to a chilled container, cover, and freeze until firm, about 6 hours or overnight.

Brown Sugar Oat Cakes

½ cup (1 stick / 113 g) unsalted butter, softened

⅓ cup packed (67 g) light brown sugar

½ teaspoon kosher salt

1 large egg, at room temperature

1 teaspoon pure vanilla extract

1 cup (132 g) all-purpose flour

¾ cup (90 g) baby rolled oats (see headnote)

Cream the butter, brown sugar, and salt in a bowl until fluffy, pressing out any lumps of brown sugar. Mix in the egg and vanilla until well combined. Add the flour and oats just until evenly mixed.

Transfer the dough to a piece of plastic wrap and use slightly moistened hands to shape it into a 6¼-inch (15 ½-cm) log with flat (not tapered) ends. Wrap the log tightly in the plastic, pressing the ends against a flat surface to flatten them. Refrigerate until firm, at least 2 hours.

About 20 minutes before baking, preheat the oven to 350°F (175°C) with racks in the upper and lower thirds of the oven. Line two baking sheets with parchment paper or silicone baking mats.

Unwrap the log and use a thin, sharp knife to shave ⅛ inch (3 mm) off of each end (press together into a cookie and bake as a snack), then cut the log into twenty-four ¼-inch-thick (6-mm) slices. Evenly space the cookies on

the prepared baking sheets and bake until the cookies are golden around the edges, about 15 minutes, rotating the pans top to bottom and front to back halfway through baking. Let the cookies cool for 5 minutes on the pan, then slide the cookies on their liners to a wire rack to cool completely.

SANDWICH!

Form sandwiches using Method #1 on page 18.

TAKE IT EASY

Use store-bought oatmeal or sugar cookies. Cook rhubarb with sugar and lime juice following the first part of the recipe instructions; let cool to room temperature, then mix into softened vanilla ice cream.

DRESS IT UP

Roll the cookies in Ginger Crumble (page 163) for authentic crumble flavor, or in a not-too-chunky oat-ginger granola.

Early Summer Sunrise

Apricot Ice Cream
on Snickerdoodles

MAKES
12
SANDWICHES

Apricots herald the beginning of the stone fruit season. As
I am crazy for them, I spun the golden orbs into both a sorbet
(page 127) and an ice cream, planning to choose the better one
for the book. I went back and forth, from tub to tub, spoonful
after spoonful, trying to decide which to exclude. Those apricots
held me in a hammerlock. There was no option but to include
both. While the sorbet is bright, fresh, and tangy, this ice cream
is round and lush. Spicy cinnamon atop the snickerdoodles
warms the golden fruit like the late afternoon sun.

Apricot Ice Cream GF

1½ pounds (680 g) ripe apricots (about
15 medium), pitted

½ cup (100 g) granulated sugar

2 tablespoons apricot preserves (optional)

½ cup (120 ml) crème fraîche (page 27),
labne, or plain Greek-style yogurt

2 teaspoons fresh lemon juice

1 cup (240 ml) heavy cream

3 tablespoons mild-flavored honey

1 tablespoon tapioca starch

¼ teaspoon kosher salt

Cut the apricots into ½-inch (1½-cm) chunks
and put them into a medium saucepan. Stir in
the sugar, preserves, if using, and 2 tablespoons
of water. Stir over medium heat until the fruit
softens, about 5 minutes. Remove from the heat
and stir in the crème fraîche and lemon juice.

Puree with an immersion blender, or in a
standard blender or food processor, until smooth.
Strain through a fine-mesh strainer into a medium
bowl, pressing on the solids to extract as much
of the flavor as possible; discard the solids.
Set aside.

Using the same saucepan, whisk the
cream, honey, tapioca, and salt until no lumps
remain. Heat the mixture over medium-high
heat, stirring with a heatproof spatula, until it
begins to steam and slightly bubble at the edges.
Adjust to a simmer and cook, stirring constantly,
until the mixture thickens to the consistency of
a cream sauce, about 90 seconds longer; do
not fully boil. Whisk the thickened milk into the
apricot mixture.

Set the bowl with the apricot mixture over a larger bowl of ice and water. Stir occasionally until the mixture is cool, taking care not to slosh water into the bowl. Cover and refrigerate until very cold, at least 2 hours. Transfer the bowl to the freezer for the last half hour before spinning it.

Freeze the mixture in an ice cream maker according to the manufacturer's directions. When it is ready, transfer the ice cream to a chilled container. Cover and freeze until firm, at least 4 hours or overnight.

Snickerdoodles

1⅓ cups (175 g) all-purpose flour

1 teaspoon baking powder

½ teaspoon kosher salt

2 tablespoons plus ⅔ cup (160 g) granulated sugar

1 teaspoon ground cinnamon

½ cup (1 stick / 113 g) unsalted butter, softened

1 large egg, at room temperature

Preheat the oven to 350°F (175°C) with a rack in the center of the oven. Line a baking sheet with parchment paper or a silicone baking mat.

Whisk together the flour, baking powder, and salt in a small bowl. Mix 2 tablespoons of the sugar with the cinnamon in a wide, shallow bowl. Set the bowls aside.

Mix the butter with the remaining ⅔ cup (134 g) sugar in a medium bowl using a wooden spoon until creamy. (Alternatively, use a handheld electric mixer or a stand mixer with the paddle attachment.) Add the egg until well mixed. Stir in the flour mixture just until no white streaks remain.

Spoon or scoop the dough by the tablespoonful to make 24 cookies, spacing them evenly on the baking sheet. Roll each scoop into a ball between your palms, then toss them in the sugar-cinnamon mixture 3 or 4 at a time to

lightly coat them, returning them to the sheet as you go.

Press the cookies with the bottom of a drinking glass to flatten them to about 2 inches (5 cm) in diameter—they will spread further as they bake. (Moisten the glass bottom or spray it with nonstick pan spray if the dough sticks.)

Bake until the cookies are nearly firm to the touch but still a bit soft, about 12 minutes, rotating the pan front to back halfway through baking.

Let the cookies cool on the pan for 5 minutes, then transfer them on their liner to a wire rack to cool completely.

SANDWICH!

Form sandwiches using Method #1 on page 18.

TAKE IT EASY

Use bakery snickerdoodles and substitute another cinnamon-friendly ice cream flavor, such as peach or honey.

DRESS IT UP

Roll the sides of the sandwiches in chopped toasted nuts or cinnamon morsels.

Plum Good

MAKES **10** SANDWICHES

Plums are the perfect sweet-tart match for tangy yogurt. Choose ripe, flavorful, red-flesh plums for deep flavor and a lush hue. I like a base of amber-flesh Santa Rosas for flavor, with a few Flavorosa, Elephant Heart, or Satsuma plums for complexity and color. Pluots will work too.

Dried lavender blossoms may be found in the spice section of some grocery stores and many natural food stores. Spicely is a good-quality brand (see Sources and Resources, page 168). To dry your own lavender, pick the blossoms from stems of culinary lavender and let them dry for several days before grinding them.

As it turns out, plums and lavender are well matched beyond their color: The lavender coaxes out pretty floral flavors from the tart plums.

Plum Frozen Yogurt GF

1½ pounds (680 g) ripe red plums, cut or pulled apart into large chunks, unpitted

⅔ cup (134 g) granulated sugar

2 tablespoons inverted sugar syrup (page 27), mild honey, or agave nectar

¼ teaspoon kosher salt

2 tablespoons tapioca starch

1 cup (227 g) plain Greek yogurt or strained yogurt (page 27), at room temperature

2 tablespoons crème de cassis or raspberry liqueur (optional)

1 teaspoon fresh lemon juice

Put the plums, sugar, syrup, salt, and ½ cup (120 ml) of water in a heavy, nonreactive medium saucepan. Bring the mixture to a lazy boil over medium heat, stirring to dissolve the sugar. Cook, stirring occasionally, until the fruit is very soft and falling apart, about 10 minutes. Strain through a medium- or fine-mesh strainer into a bowl, pressing on the solids until only pits and skins remain; discard the solids. Return the purée to the saucepan.

Stir the tapioca with 1 tablespoon of water to make a smooth paste, then add the paste to the saucepan. Heat the mixture over medium-high heat, stirring with a heatproof spatula, until it begins to steam and slightly bubble at the edges. Adjust to a simmer and cook, stirring

constantly, until the mixture thickens to the consistency of a cream sauce, about 2 minutes longer; do not fully boil. Remove from the heat.

Whisk the yogurt, cassis, if using, and lemon juice in a medium metal bowl until smooth. Whisk in about ½ cup (120 ml) of the thickened plum mixture until smooth, then whisk in the remaining plum mixture.

Set the bowl over a larger bowl of ice and water. Stir occasionally until the mixture is cool, taking care not to slosh water into the bowl. Cover and refrigerate until very cold, at least 2 hours. Transfer the bowl to the freezer for the last half hour before spinning it.

Freeze the mixture in an ice cream maker according to the manufacturer's directions. While the ice cream spins, line a 9-inch (23-cm) square baking pan with waxed paper and place it in the freezer. When the ice cream is ready, spread it evenly into the prepared pan, cover with plastic wrap, pressing it directly against the surface, and freeze until firm, at least 6 hours or overnight.

Lavender-Walnut Shortbread

½ cup (100 g) granulated sugar

1 teaspoon dried lavender blossoms

½ cup (1 stick / 113 g) unsalted butter, softened

¼ teaspoon kosher salt

½ cup (55 g) toasted walnuts (see page 25)

1 cup (132 g) all-purpose flour

1 to 2 tablespoons turbinado or other coarse sugar

Preheat the oven to 350°F (175°C) with a rack in the center of the oven. Line a baking sheet with a silicone baking mat or parchment paper.

Process the sugar and lavender blossoms in a food processor until the sugar has the texture of powdered sugar. (Take care as you open the processor to avoid inhaling a cloud of scented sugar.) Add the butter and salt and process until

smooth and creamy, about 1 minute, scraping down the bowl as needed. Add the walnuts and pulse several times until the nuts are medium fine. Add the flour and process until the mixture balls up around the blade.

Divide the dough into 20 equal pieces, rolling each piece into a ball between your palms. Put the turbinado sugar in a medium bowl and drop in a few of the balls, tossing to coat them in the sugar. Evenly space the dough balls on the baking sheet. Continue until all of the balls have been coated. Use a flat-bottomed drinking glass to flatten the balls into 2½-inch (6-cm) rounds. (Moisten the glass bottom or spray it with non-stick pan spray if the dough sticks.)

Bake until the cookies begin to color around the edges, about 13 minutes, rotating the pan front to back halfway through baking. Transfer the cookies on their liner to a wire rack to cool completely.

SANDWICH!

Form sandwiches using Method #3 on page 19, using a 2½-inch (6-cm) cutter to cut out 10 rounds of the frozen yogurt, gathering scraps to form the last round or two, if needed. Alternatively, form sandwiches using Method #1.

TAKE IT EASY

Use store-bought shortbread or walnut cookies and stir ½ teaspoon finely ground lavender blossoms into softened plum frozen yogurt, ice cream, or sorbet, or vanilla ice cream.

DRESS IT UP

Roll the sides of the sandwiches in a pinch of lavender ground in a spice grinder, mixed with colored sugar.

Peachy Keen

Peaches and Cream Ice Cream
on Oatmeal Cookies

MAKES
12
SANDWICHES

Nothing says summer like a dripping, velvet-skinned peach. This sandwich captures the peach's essence, though it is melting ice cream that will be dribbling down your chin rather than peach juice. The oatmeal cookies can be made with gluten-free oat flour for a gluten-free sandwich.

Leaving the peach skins on gives the ice cream a rosy glow. If you prefer to peel them, you can skip the straining step.

Peaches and Cream Ice Cream GF

1½ pounds (680 g) ripe peaches, about
5 medium peaches, pitted and cut into ½-inch
(1½-cm) chunks

⅔ cup (134 g) granulated sugar

1 teaspoon fresh lemon juice

¼ teaspoon kosher salt

¾ cup (180 ml) heavy cream

1½ tablespoons mild-flavored honey, such as
clover or orange blossom

1 tablespoon tapioca starch

⅔ cup (160 ml) crème fraîche (page 27), labne, or
plain Greek-style whole-milk yogurt, stirred smooth

½ teaspoon pure vanilla extract

Stir together the peaches, sugar, lemon juice, and salt in a bowl. Set aside to get juicy.

Whisk the cream, honey, and tapioca in a medium saucepan until no lumps remain. Heat the mixture over medium-high heat, stirring with a heatproof spatula, until it begins to steam and slightly bubble at the edges. Adjust to a simmer and cook, stirring constantly, until the mixture thickens to the consistency of a cream sauce, about 1 minute longer; do not fully boil. Transfer the mixture to a medium metal bowl, then nest the bowl inside a larger bowl of ice and water until cool, taking care not to slosh water into the mixture.

While the mixture cools, process the peaches with all of their juices in a blender or food processor until smooth. Strain through a standard or fine-mesh strainer into a bowl; discard the solids. Remove the cooled milk from the ice bath and stir in the peaches, crème fraîche, and vanilla until smooth. Cover and refrigerate until very cold, at least 2 hours. Transfer the bowl to the freezer for the last half hour before spinning it.

Freeze the mixture in an ice cream maker according to the manufacturer's directions.

When it is ready, transfer the ice cream to a chilled container. Cover and freeze until firm, at least 4 hours or overnight.

Oatmeal Cookies GF OPTION

¾ cup (100 g) white whole wheat, whole wheat, or oat flour

½ teaspoon baking soda

½ teaspoon baking powder

½ teaspoon kosher salt

½ cup (1 stick / 113 g) unsalted butter, softened

⅔ cup packed (134 g) light brown sugar

1 large egg

½ teaspoon pure vanilla extract

1½ cups (180 g) rolled oats

½ cup (80 g) raisins (optional)

Preheat the oven to 350°F (175ºC) with racks in the upper and lower thirds of the oven. Line two baking sheets with parchment paper or silicone baking mats. Whisk together the flour, baking soda, baking powder, and salt in a small bowl.

Put the butter and brown sugar in a mixing bowl and use a wooden spoon or a handheld electric mixer to mix until they are creamy. Add the egg and vanilla and mix until smooth. Stir in the flour mixture just until everything is well combined, then stir in the oats and raisins, if using.

Spoon or scoop the batter in tablespoons onto the prepared baking sheets, spacing them evenly, to make 24 cookies. Press the cookies with lightly dampened fingers to flatten them slightly—they will spread further as they bake. Bake until the cookies are light golden around the edges, 8 to 10 minutes, rotating the pans top to bottom and front to back halfway through baking.

Let the cookies cool on the pan for 5 minutes, then transfer them directly to a wire rack to cool completely, sliding a spatula under them if they do not release easily.

SANDWICH!

Form sandwiches using Method #1 on page 18, using ¼ to ⅓ cup (60 to 80 ml) of ice cream per sandwich.

TAKE IT EASY

Use store-bought oatmeal cookies and peach ice cream.

DRESS IT UP

Roll the sides of the sandwiches in chopped toasted pecans or walnuts, chopped crystalized ginger, or Ginger Crumble (page 163).

Berry Pavlova

Blackberry-Buttermilk
Ice Cream on Crispy-Chewy
Meringues

MAKES 12 SANDWICHES

Have you had a pavlova, the ethereal dessert of meringue shells topped with fruit and cream, created by an Australian pastry chef in honor of a Russian ballerina? In this interpretation, meringue cookies encase a tangy buttermilk ice cream with captivating citrus-herbal flavor from lemon verbena. The fruits take the form of a sweet-tart berry swirl.

Look for lemon verbena plants at your local nursery. Be sure your bowl and beaters are sparkling clean when whipping the egg whites for the best volume. Vinegar gives the snow-white meringue its classic chewy center.

Blackberry-Buttermilk Ice Cream GF

1½ cups (360 ml) heavy cream

½ cup (100 g) granulated sugar

¼ teaspoon kosher salt

⅓ cup packed (12 g) fresh lemon verbena leaves, or one 1-by-3-inch (2½-by-7½-cm) strip of lemon peel, yellow part only

5 teaspoons tapioca starch

¼ cup (84 g) mild-flavored honey

1 cup (240 ml) buttermilk, full-fat or low-fat

¼ cup (60 ml) fresh lemon juice, from Meyer lemons if available

1 recipe Berry Ribbon (page 159), made with blackberries

Stir the cream, sugar, and salt in a medium saucepan over medium heat until it steams and bubbles at the edges; do not boil. Stir in the leaves (or lemon peel), completely submerging them, and let stand off the heat for 20 minutes.

Put the tapioca and honey in a medium bowl and strain about ½ cup (120 ml) of the infused milk into the mixture, stirring until no lumps remain. Strain in the rest of the infused milk, pressing on the leaves to extract their flavor; discard the leaves.

Return the mixture to the saucepan and bring to just below a boil over medium heat, stirring with a heatproof spatula. Adjust to a simmer and cook, stirring constantly, until the mixture thickens to the consistency of a cream sauce, about 2 minutes longer; do not fully boil. Remove from the heat, transfer the mixture back to the bowl, and stir in the buttermilk and lemon juice.

Set the bowl over a larger bowl of ice and water, and stir occasionally until the mixture is cool, taking care not to slosh water into the bowl. Cover and refrigerate until very cold, at least 2 hours. Transfer the bowl to the freezer for the last half hour before spinning it.

Freeze the mixture in an ice cream maker according to the manufacturer's directions. While the ice cream spins, line a 13-by-9-inch (33-by-23-cm) baking pan with waxed paper and place it in the freezer. When the ice cream is ready, spread it evenly into the prepared pan, swirling it with the Berry Ribbon as you pack the ice cream into the container (see page 156). Cover with plastic wrap, pressing it directly against the surface, and freeze until firm, at least 6 hours or overnight.

Crispy-Chewy Meringues GF DF

Neutral vegetable oil, for the parchment

4 large egg whites, at room temperature

⅛ teaspoon cream of tartar

⅛ teaspoon fine sea salt

1 cup superfine or granulated sugar

1 tablespoon distilled white vinegar

Preheat the oven to 225°F (110°C) with racks in the upper and lower thirds of the oven. Line two rimmed baking sheets with parchment paper. Draw twelve 3-inch (7½-cm) rounds on the reverse side of each sheet to use as a guide for piping the meringues, then flip the parchments back over onto the baking sheets with the writing underneath. Rub about 1 teaspoon of oil all over each parchment sheet.

In the bowl of a stand mixer fitted with the whisk attachment, beat the egg whites, cream of tartar, and salt at medium speed until the whites hold soft peaks. With the mixer running, add the sugar, about 1 tablespoon at a time, pausing after each addition to fully incorporate it and occasionally stopping to scrape down the bowl. Increase the speed to medium-high and beat until the whites form firm, shiny peaks that hold their shape and curl over just slightly when you

invert the beater, a few minutes longer. Add the vinegar at low speed.

Using a pastry bag fitted with a ½-inch (1½-cm) round tip (or a zipper-top bag with a ½-inch / 1½-cm opening cut in one corner), pipe out the meringue, starting at the center of each marked round on the parchment paper and spiraling toward the outer edge. (Alternatively, make 24 mounds and use the back of the spoon to form rounds.) Use the back of a spoon to make pretty swirls in the meringue if you wish.

Bake until the shells feel dry and no longer sticky to the touch, 50 to 60 minutes, rotating the pans top to bottom and front to back halfway through baking. They should remain white; if they threaten to brown, reduce the oven to 175°F (79°C) to finish baking. Turn off the oven with the baking sheets inside and the oven door closed and leave the shells inside until they are completely cool, at least 2 hours or up to 1 day.

SANDWICH!

Form sandwiches using Method #3 on page 19, using a 3-inch (7½-cm) cutter to cut out 12 rounds of the ice cream, gathering scraps to form the last round or two, if needed. These sandwiches are best enjoyed up to 48 hours after filling them. For longer storage, freeze the ice cream and meringues separately and form the sandwiches shortly before serving them.

TAKE IT EASY

Use store-bought meringues. Swirl lemon curd into softened blackberry ice cream, or swirl Berry Ribbon (page 159) into lemon ice cream.

DRESS IT UP

Spread Lemon Curd (page 160) on the meringues before filling with the ice cream.

Blueberry Muffin

Blueberry Sorbet on Blueberry Muffin Top Cookies

MAKES 12 SANDWICHES

This sandwich includes everything I love about blueberry muffins: vibrant blue color and deep berry flavor in the sorbet, with dried blueberries in the cookies to double the pleasure.

The muffin tops make the sandwich feel a bit like a frozen whoopie pie. This one really benefits from several minutes to soften at room temperature before eating, in which time the cookies go from frozen hard to soft muffin-y goodness.

Blueberry Sorbet GF DF

2 pints (700 g) fresh or frozen (thawed) blueberries

¼ cup (60 ml) inverted sugar syrup (page 27), golden syrup, or agave nectar

¼ cup (50 g) granulated sugar

2 tablespoons blueberry preserves (optional)

1 tablespoon fresh lime or lemon juice

Pinch of salt

Process all of the ingredients in a food processor or blender until very smooth. Strain the mixture through a fine-mesh strainer into a bowl, pressing on the solids to extract as much flavor as possible.

Cover and refrigerate until very cold, about 2 hours. Transfer the bowl to the freezer for the last half hour before spinning it. Freeze in an ice cream maker according to the manufacturer's directions.

While the sorbet spins, line a 13-by-9-inch (33-by-23-cm) baking pan with waxed paper and place it in the freezer. When the sorbet is ready, spread it evenly into the prepared pan, cover with plastic wrap, pressing it directly against the surface, and freeze until firm, at least 4 hours or overnight.

Blueberry Muffin Top Cookies

½ cup (60 g) dried blueberries

1½ cups (200 g) all-purpose flour

1 teaspoon baking powder

½ teaspoon kosher salt

½ cup (1 stick / 113 g) unsalted butter

¾ cup (150 g) granulated sugar

¼ cup (60 ml) whole milk

1 large egg

½ teaspoon pure vanilla extract

½ teaspoon packed finely grated lemon zest

2 tablespoons brown sugar

¼ teaspoon ground cinnamon

Preheat the oven to 375°F (190°C) with racks in the upper and lower thirds of the oven. Line two baking sheets with parchment paper or silicone baking mats.

Put the blueberries in a bowl and cover with boiling water to plump them. Whisk the flour, baking powder, and salt in a small bowl. Set both bowls aside.

Melt the butter in a large saucepan. Remove from the heat and stir in the sugar. Add the milk, egg, vanilla, and lemon zest, stirring until well mixed. Stir in the flour mixture until only a few white streaks remain. Drain the blueberries, shaking off excess water, and gently fold them into the batter.

Stir the brown sugar and cinnamon together in a small bowl.

Scoop 24 balls of the mixture in rounded tablespoons, spacing them evenly on the baking sheets. Sprinkle the tops with the cinnamon-sugar.

Bake until the cookies are barely firm to the touch and just beginning to turn light golden around the edges, 10 to 12 minutes, rotating the pans top to bottom and front to back halfway through baking. Let the cookies cool for 5 minutes on the sheets, then slide the cookies on the parchment to wire racks to cool completely.

SANDWICH!

Form sandwiches using Method #3 on page 19, using a 2½-inch (6-cm) cutter to cut out 12 rounds of the sorbet, gathering scraps to form the last round or two, if needed. Alternatively, form sandwiches using Method #1.

TAKE IT EASY

Use store-bought blueberry muffin tops and blueberry sorbet.

DRESS IT UP

Roll the sides of the sandwiches in Ginger Crumble (page 163), similar to a streusel muffin topping, or in chopped crystallized ginger or ginger granola.

Lemon Zinger

Lemon Curd Ice Cream on
Soft Ginger Cookies

MAKES
12
SANDWICHES

I don't often make custard-based ice creams, but here, the yolks already used to thicken the lemon curd eliminate the need to use other thickeners—the curd serves as flavoring and thickener all at once. The boldly spiced cookies perfectly complement the rich-tart curd.

Note that the cookies use two whites and the curd two yolks. Coincidence? No way.

Lemon Curd Ice Cream GF

1 recipe Lemon Curd (page 160), cooled to room temperature or chilled

1 cup (240 ml) heavy cream

1¼ cups (300 ml) whole milk

Whisk the cream and milk into the curd.

Cover and refrigerate until very cold, at least 2 hours. Transfer the bowl to the freezer for the last half hour before spinning it.

Freeze the mixture in an ice cream maker according to the manufacturer's directions. When it is ready, transfer the ice cream to a chilled container. Cover and freeze until firm, at least 4 hours or overnight.

Soft Ginger Cookies

2 cups (264 g) all-purpose flour

1½ teaspoons baking soda

2 teaspoons ground ginger

½ teaspoon ground cinnamon

¼ teaspoon kosher salt

¼ teaspoon ground cardamom (optional)

A few twists of finely ground black pepper (optional)

½ cup (1 stick / 113 g) unsalted butter, softened

¾ cup packed (150 g) light brown sugar

¼ cup (50 g) granulated sugar

¼ cup (60 ml) molasses

2 large egg whites

2 tablespoons turbinado or coarse sugar, for rolling

Whisk the flour, baking soda, ginger, cinnamon, and salt in a small bowl. Whisk in the cardamom and pepper, if using. Set aside.

Mix the butter with the brown and granulated sugars in a medium bowl using a wooden spoon until they are well blended. Stir in the molasses, then the egg whites, mixing well and scraping the bowl with a spatula between additions. Stir in the flour mixture until no white streaks remain. Refrigerate until firm enough to form balls of the mixture, at least 1 hour.

Preheat the oven to 350°F (175°C) with racks in the upper and lower thirds of the oven. Line two baking sheets with parchment paper or silicone baking mats.

Put the turbinado sugar for rolling in a bowl. Use a scoop or your hands to form 24 balls using a rounded tablespoon of dough per cookie. As you make the balls, dunk one side in the sugar, then place sugar-side up on the baking sheet, evenly spacing the cookies with about 1 inch (2½ cm) all around them.

Bake until the cookies are just set, 10 to 12 minutes, rotating the pans top to bottom and front to back halfway through baking. The cookies will be puffed when you pull them from the oven and will settle as they cool. Let the cookies cool on the pans for 10 minutes, then transfer them on their liners to wire racks to cool completely.

SANDWICH!

Form sandwiches using Method #1 on page 18, using about ¼ to ⅓ cup (60 to 80 ml) of ice cream per sandwich. Alternatively, form the sandwiches using a 2-inch-tall (5-cm) cutter as a mold following Method #2.

TAKE IT EASY

Use store-bought, bakery-style soft ginger cookies. Stir or swirl store-bought or homemade lemon curd (page 160) into softened vanilla ice cream.

DRESS IT UP

Roll the sandwiches in finely chopped crystallized ginger or candied lemon peel.

Dreamsicle

Orange Sherbet on
Vanilla-Orange Wafers

MAKES 12 SANDWICHES

Oranges are a winter fruit that taste like summer, just right for remembering sunshine in the depths of the cold. These orange-vanilla sandwiches remind me of a Creamsicle, an ice pop that may taste great to a ten-year-old, but bears little resemblance to real citrus and vanilla. This is the one I dream of, with a bit of orange in the cookie echoing the sherbet.

I love sherbet for its light interpretation of ice cream. With a hint of richness from milk but no cream or eggs, it's the happy medium between ice cream and sorbet. Choose unwaxed, organic, or pesticide-free oranges, as you will be using the rind in both the sherbet and the wafers. To vary the flavor, consider substituting blood oranges or mandarins for the oranges.

Orange Sherbet GF

1 cup (240 ml) whole milk

¾ cup (150 g) granulated sugar

2 tablespoons inverted sugar syrup (page 27), golden syrup, or light agave nectar

1 tablespoon tapioca starch

¼ teaspoon kosher salt

Zest of 2 oranges, outer orange part only, cut in wide strips with a vegetable peeler

2 cups (480 ml) fresh orange juice

1 tablespoon fresh lemon juice

¾ teaspoon pure vanilla extract

2 tablespoons mandarin or plain vodka (optional)

Whisk ½ cup (120 ml) of the milk with the sugar, syrup, tapioca, and salt in a medium saucepan until no lumps remain. Stir in the remaining ½ cup (120 ml) milk. Heat the mixture over medium-high heat, stirring with a heatproof spatula, until it begins to steam and slightly bubble at the edges. Adjust to a simmer and cook, stirring constantly, until the mixture thickens to the consistency of a cream sauce, about 1 minute longer; do not fully boil.

Transfer the mixture to a metal bowl and stir in the orange zest and juice, lemon juice, vanilla, and vodka, if using, until everything is well combined.

Set the bowl over a larger bowl of ice and water and stir occasionally until the mixture is cool, taking care not to slosh water into the bowl.

Cover and refrigerate until very cold, at least 2 hours. Transfer the bowl to the freezer for the last half hour before spinning it.

Strain the mixture, pressing on the rind to release its flavorful oils; discard the rind. Freeze in an ice cream maker according to the manufacturer's directions. When it is ready, transfer the sherbet to a chilled container and freeze until firm, at least 6 hours or overnight.

Vanilla-Orange Wafers

1¾ cups (230 g) unbleached all-purpose flour

½ teaspoon baking soda

¼ teaspoon kosher salt

½ cup (1 stick / 113 g) unsalted butter, softened

½ cup (100 g) granulated sugar

Finely grated zest of 1 orange

2 tablespoons fresh orange juice

2 tablespoons inverted sugar syrup (page 27) or light agave nectar

½ teaspoon pure vanilla extract

2 tablespoons coarse or granulated sugar

Preheat the oven to 325°F (165°C) with racks in the upper and lower thirds of the oven. Line two baking sheets with parchment paper or silicone baking mats.

Whisk the flour, baking soda, and salt in a small bowl; set aside.

In a stand mixer fitted with the paddle attachment, mix the butter and granulated sugar on medium-high speed until light, about 3 minutes, scraping the bowl as needed. Mix in the orange zest and juice, syrup, and vanilla on low speed. Mix in the flour mixture just until no streaks of flour are visible.

Divide the dough into 24 pieces using 1 tablespoon of dough for each, rolling each into a ball between your palms. Put the coarse sugar in a medium bowl and drop in the balls, 6 at a time, tossing to coat them in the sugar. Evenly space the dough balls on the baking sheets. Flatten each ball with the bottom of a drinking glass into a 2½-inch (6-cm) round. (Moisten the glass bottom or spray it with nonstick pan spray if the dough sticks.) The edges will fray a bit, which looks pretty.

Bake until the cookies begin to color around the edges, 8 to 10 minutes, rotating the racks top to bottom and front to back halfway through baking. Let the cookies cool on the sheets for 5 minutes, then transfer them directly to wire racks to cool completely.

SANDWICH!

Form sandwiches using Method #1 on page 18, using ¼ cup (60 ml) of sherbet per sandwich.

TAKE IT EASY

Use store-bought orange or vanilla cookies and orange sherbet. Or soften 1 pint (480 ml) each of orange sherbet or sorbet and vanilla ice cream, and swirl the two together.

DRESS IT UP

Dip the sandwiches in Chocolate Shell (page 165), or roll them in mini chocolate chips.

Hawaiian Holiday

Piña Colada Sorbet on
Macadamia Cookies

MAKES
10
SANDWICHES

Packed with the favorite tastes of Hawaii, this is a mini-vacation in a sandwich. Use the refrigerated or shelf-stable type of coconut beverage for a light-textured sorbet, or canned coconut milk for a richer one. In addition to adding tropical flavor, the rum helps keep the sorbet from freezing hard. Pure coconut extract, my preference, boosts the sorbet's flavor without adding the "suntan lotion" taste of artificial extract, which some people associate with classic piña colada flavor. With no extract, the flavor comes predominantly from the pineapple, with a subtle hint of coconut from the milk.

Piña Colada Sorbet GF DF

3½ cups (600 g) 1-inch (2½-cm) pineapple chunks, cut from a ripe pineapple

3 tablespoons packed brown sugar, dark or light

1 cup (240 ml) unsweetened coconut milk, shelf-stable or canned, plus more if needed

3 tablespoons golden syrup, inverted sugar syrup (page 27), or agave nectar

2 teaspoons fresh lime juice

1 tablespoon rum, dark or light (optional)

¼ teaspoon coconut extract (optional)

¼ teaspoon kosher salt

Preheat the oven to 450°F (230°C) with a rack in the center of the oven. Line a baking sheet with parchment paper or a silicone baking mat.

Place the pineapple chunks in a single layer on the baking sheet and crumble the brown sugar over them; toss to coat. Roast the pineapple in the oven until the sugar melts and begins to brown, about 10 minutes.

Scrape the pineapple and as much of its syrupy juices as you can collect into a food processor or blender. Add the coconut milk and the golden syrup; process until smooth. Strain the mixture through a regular-mesh strainer into a bowl, pressing on the solids to extract as much flavor as possible; discard the solids.

Measure the pineapple mixture and add more coconut milk, if needed, to make 3 cups (720 ml). (It's fine to use all of the pineapple mixture if it measures only a bit more.)

Stir in the lime juice, rum (if using), coconut extract (if using), and salt.

Cover and refrigerate until very cold, at least 2 hours. Transfer the bowl to the freezer for the last half hour before spinning it.

Freeze the sorbet in an ice cream maker according to the manufacturer's directions. While the sorbet spins, line a 9-inch (23-cm) square baking pan with waxed paper and place it in the freezer. When the sorbet is ready, spread it evenly into the prepared pan, cover with plastic wrap, pressing it directly against the surface, and freeze until firm, about 6 hours or overnight.

Macadamia Cookies

½ cup (70 g) macadamia nuts, toasted and cooled (see page 25)

½ cup (1 stick / 113 g) unsalted butter, softened

⅓ cup (40 g) powdered sugar

1 cup (132 g) all-purpose flour

¼ teaspoon kosher salt

2 tablespoons turbinado or other coarse sugar, for rolling

Pulse the nuts in a food processor to coarsely chop them. Add the butter and powdered sugar and process until creamy, about 1 minute, stopping to scrape down the bowl as needed. Add the flour and salt, pulsing several times until the dough is well blended. The dough should hold together when you press it between your fingers.

Transfer the dough to a lightly floured surface and bring it together into a mass, then shape it into a 5¼-inch (13-cm) log with flat (not tapered) ends.

Lay a sheet of plastic wrap on a flat surface and sprinkle it with the turbinado sugar. Roll the log across the sugar, pressing it into the sugar to coat it evenly. Wrap the log tightly, press the ends against a flat surface to flatten them, and refrigerate until very firm, about 2 hours, or freeze for 30 minutes.

About 20 minutes before baking, preheat the oven to 350°F (175°C) with racks in the upper and lower thirds of the oven. Line two baking sheets with parchment paper or silicone baking mats.

Unwrap the log and use a thin, sharp knife to shave ⅛ inch (3 mm) off of each end (press together into a cookie and bake as a snack), then cut the log into twenty ¼-inch-thick (6-mm) slices. Evenly space the cookies on the prepared baking sheets and bake until the cookies begin to color around the edges, 13 to 15 minutes, rotating the pans top to bottom and front to back halfway through baking. Let the cookies cool on the pans for 5 minutes, then slide the cookies on their liners to a wire rack to cool completely.

SANDWICH!

Form sandwiches using Method #3 on page 19, using a 2½-inch (6-cm) cutter to cut out 10 rounds of the sorbet, gathering scraps to form the last round or two, if needed. Alternatively, form sandwiches using Method #1.

TAKE IT EASY

Use store-bought macadamia nut cookies. Fold drained, crushed pineapple into coconut sorbet, or stir coconut extract into pineapple sorbet.

DRESS IT UP

Roll the sides of the sandwiches in chopped toasted macadamia nuts or shredded coconut, toasted or not.

Got Your Goat

Frozen Honey-Vanilla Goat's Milk on Sugar Cone Cookies

MAKES 12 SANDWICHES

This ice milk charms with its light texture and mild, earthy taste from goat's milk and honey. The flavor comes predominantly from the honey, so choose one you really enjoy, with mild to moderate intensity. Also, seek out fresh, local goat's milk—here in Northern California I get mine from Redwood Hill Farm in Sebastopol, California, where I observed the Bice family and their crew talking to each of the goats in their happy-looking, floppy-eared herd by name. For a richer ice cream, substitute up to a cup of heavy cream for an equal amount of goat's milk, stirring it in after the mixture has thickened, or use crème fraîche in place of the yogurt.

Frozen Honey-Vanilla Goat's Milk GF

3 cups (720 ml) goat's milk

½ cup (120 ml) honey

3 tablespoons tapioca starch

¼ teaspoon kosher salt

1 vanilla bean, split

2 tablespoons plain goat's milk yogurt or Greek (cow's milk) yogurt

Pour ½ cup (120 ml) of the milk into a medium saucepan. Whisk in the honey, tapioca, and salt until no lumps remain. Stir in the remaining 2½ cups (600 ml) of milk. Scrape the seeds from the vanilla pod into the milk and drop in the pod as well.

Heat the mixture over medium-high heat, stirring with a heatproof spatula, until it begins to steam and slightly bubble at the edges. Adjust to a simmer and cook, stirring constantly, until the mixture thickens to the consistency of a cream sauce, about 2 minutes longer; do not fully boil. Remove from the heat.

Transfer the mixture to a metal bowl set over a larger bowl of ice and water. Stir occasionally until the mixture is cool, taking care not to slosh water into the bowl. Cover and refrigerate until very cold, at least 2 hours. Transfer the bowl to the freezer for the last half hour before spinning it.

Remove the vanilla pod (discard or rinse and save for another use; see page 26). Stir the yogurt with a small amount of the goat's milk mixture until smooth, then stir back into the mixture. Freeze in an ice cream maker according to the manufacturer's directions.

While the ice milk spins, line a 13-by-9-inch (33-by-23-cm) baking pan with waxed paper or plastic wrap and place it in the freezer. When the ice milk is ready, spread it evenly into the prepared pan, cover with plastic wrap, pressing it directly against the surface, and freeze until firm, at least 4 hours or overnight.

Sugar Cone Cookies

1 cup (132 g) all-purpose flour

1 teaspoon baking powder

¼ teaspoon kosher salt

2 large eggs

½ cup (100 g) granulated sugar

6 tablespoons (85 g) unsalted butter, melted and cooled

1 teaspoon pure vanilla extract

Preheat the oven to 350°F (175°C) with racks in the upper and lower thirds of the oven. Line two rimless baking sheets with parchment paper.

Whisk the flour, baking powder, and salt in a small bowl; set aside.

Beat the eggs with the sugar on medium-high speed using a stand mixer fitted with the whisk attachment until the eggs are thick and light, about 5 minutes. With the mixer on low speed, add the butter in a slow stream, then the vanilla. Add the flour mixture just until no white streaks remain. (Alternatively, use a handheld electric mixer.)

Drop the batter in scant tablespoons onto the baking sheet to make 12 cookies on each sheet, leaving plenty of room all around to spread them. Use a small offset spatula to spread each cookie into a neat 2½-inch (6-cm) round.

Bake until the cookies are golden a bit beyond the edges, about 15 minutes, rotating the pans top to bottom and front to back halfway through baking.

Slide the cookies on their liners onto a flat surface. For neat rounds, cut the cookies with 2½- to 3-inch (5- to 7½-cm) cutters while they are still warm. Transfer the cookies to a wire rack to cool completely.

SANDWICH!

Form sandwiches using Method #3 on page 19, using a 2½-inch (6-cm) cutter to cut out 12 rounds of the ice milk, gathering scraps to form the last round or two, if needed. Alternatively, form sandwiches using Method #1.

TAKE IT EASY

Use store-bought pizzelle or sugar cookies in place of the sugar cone cookies. If you can find goat's milk ice cream in your area (Laloo's is a great brand), substitute any flavor you like.

DRESS IT UP

Roll the sides of the sandwiches in chopped toasted nuts, nut brittle, or granola.

Got Your Goat (pages 88–89)

5

World View

Ice cream sandwiches offer a nonpareil playground for exploring the flavors of the world, one bite at a time, with infinite combinations of flavors and textures in the cookies, fillings, and decorations. This chapter takes a quick spin around the globe, through Asia, Africa, Europe, and Latin America, picking up favorite flavors along the way.

Top Banana (page 92)

Top Banana

Caribbean Banana Ice Cream
on Peanut Butter Cookies

MAKES
12
SANDWICHES

Who can resist a peanut butter and banana sandwich? Especially when the bananas are broiled into caramelized submission with brown sugar, rum, and lime, then sandwiched between chewy peanut butter cookies? Sounds like lunchtime to me.

Caribbean Banana Ice Cream GF

3 ripe bananas, peeled and cut in half lengthwise

½ cup packed (100 g) light brown sugar

1 teaspoon packed finely grated lime zest

1 tablespoon unsalted butter

2 teaspoons fresh lime juice

1 tablespoon dark rum (optional)

1½ cups (360 ml) whole milk

2 tablespoons tapioca starch

2 tablespoons mild-flavored honey, golden syrup, or agave nectar

¼ teaspoon kosher salt

1 cup (240 ml) heavy cream

Preheat the broiler to high with a rack 6 to 8 inches (15 to 20 cm) from the heat. Line a rimmed baking sheet with foil.

Place the bananas cut-side up on the baking sheet and sprinkle ¼ cup (50 g) of the brown sugar and all of the lime zest evenly over them. Dot the bananas with the butter and drizzle the lime juice and rum, if using, over the tops. Broil until the sauce is bubbly and the bananas are golden in places, 3 to 5 minutes, stirring the bananas and sauce about halfway through. Set aside to cool.

Whisk ½ cup (120 ml) of the milk with the tapioca, honey, and salt in a large saucepan until no lumps remain. Stir in the remaining 1 cup (240 ml) milk and the remaining ¼ cup (50 g) brown sugar. Heat the mixture over medium-high heat, stirring with a heatproof spatula, until it begins to steam and slightly bubble at the edges. Adjust to a simmer and cook, stirring constantly, until the mixture thickens to the consistency of a cream sauce, about 2 minutes longer; do not fully boil.

Remove from the heat and stir in the cream. Break up the bananas into chunks and add them with all of their sauce. Process with an immersion blender until completely smooth. (Alternatively, process in a blender.)

Transfer the mixture to a metal bowl set over a larger bowl of ice and water. Stir occasionally until the mixture is cool, taking care not to slosh water into the bowl. Cover and refrigerate until very cold, at least 2 hours. Transfer the bowl to the freezer for the last half hour before spinning it.

Freeze the mixture in an ice cream maker according to the manufacturer's directions. When it is ready, transfer the ice cream to a chilled container, cover, and freeze until firm, at least 6 hours or overnight.

Peanut Butter Cookies

½ cup (1 stick / 113 g) unsalted butter, softened

½ cup (128 g) creamy natural-style peanut butter

⅓ cup packed (67 g) light brown sugar

⅓ cup (67 g) granulated sugar

½ teaspoon kosher salt

1 large egg

½ teaspoon pure vanilla extract

1 cup (132 g) all-purpose flour

¼ teaspoon baking soda

Preheat the oven to 350°F (175°C) with racks in the upper and lower thirds of the oven. Line two baking sheets with parchment paper or silicone baking mats.

Process the butter, peanut butter, brown and granulated sugars, and salt in a food processor until smooth and well combined. Scrape down the bowl, then add the egg and vanilla and process again until smooth. Stir the baking soda into the flour, then add to the processor and process until the dough clumps together around the blade. (Alternatively, use a handheld electric or stand mixer with the paddle attachment, or a wooden spoon.)

Scoop 12 cookies onto each sheet using a 1-tablespoon scoop, spacing them evenly with room to spread. (Alternatively, spoon or pinch off tablespoon-size pieces of dough, rolling each between your palms to make a ball.) Press the tops of the cookies with a fork in two directions to flatten them and form a crosshatch pattern.

Bake until the cookies are puffy and softly set, about 10 minutes, rotating the pans top to bottom and front to back halfway through the baking time. The bottoms will be light golden but the tops will be pale. (The cookies will firm as they cool.) Let the cookies cool on the pans for 5 minutes, then transfer them on their liners to wire racks to cool completely.

SANDWICH!

Form sandwiches using Method #1 on page 18, using ¼ to ⅓ cup (60 to 80 ml) of ice cream per sandwich.

TAKE IT EASY

Use bakery-style soft peanut butter cookies, or serve the ice cream between slices of banana bread. Prepare and broil the bananas following the instructions above; smash with a fork, cool to room temperature, and stir into softened vanilla ice cream.

DRESS IT UP

Roll the sandwiches in Honey-Roasted Peanut Brittle (page 162), or stir the chopped brittle into the ice cream during the last minute of spinning.

Latin Love

Dulce de Leche Ice Cream on
Brown Butter Blondies

MAKES
12
SANDWICHES

With rich caramel echoed at every level, this one is all about extravagance. You could use store-bought dulce de leche to flavor the ice cream or make it using sweetened condensed milk, but making it yourself from fresh milk, while it takes a bit of patience, is easy and fun and immensely more complex and flavorful.

Flaunting nutty browned butter, the blondies are the perfect complement, and they could hardly be easier to make. Dark brown sugar contributes an extra layer of caramelized flavor, but light brown sugar will work too.

Dulce de Leche Ice Cream GF

1 cup (240 ml) whole milk

2 tablespoons tapioca starch

¼ teaspoon kosher salt

1 cup (240 ml) heavy cream

1 cup (240 ml) Dulce de Leche (page 158)

2 tablespoons strained yogurt (page 27), labne, or plain Greek yogurt, at room temperature

1 teaspoon pure vanilla extract

Whisk ½ cup (120 ml) of the milk with the tapioca and salt in a in a medium saucepan until no lumps remain. Stir in the remaining ½ cup (120 ml) milk and the cream. Heat the mixture over medium-high heat, stirring with a heatproof spatula, until it begins to steam and slightly bubble at the edges. Adjust to a simmer and cook, stirring constantly, until the mixture thickens to the consistency of a cream sauce, about 2 minutes longer; do not fully boil. Set aside.

Whisk the dulce de leche, yogurt, and vanilla in a medium bowl until completely smooth. Whisk in the thickened milk just to combine.

Set the bowl with the ice cream mixture over a larger bowl of ice and water. Stir occasionally until the mixture is cool, taking care not to slosh water into the bowl. Cover and refrigerate until very cold, at least 2 hours. Transfer the bowl to the freezer for the last half hour before spinning it.

Freeze the mixture in an ice cream maker according to the manufacturer's directions. Transfer the ice cream to a chilled container, cover, and freeze until firm but still spreadable, about 4 hours.

Brown Butter Blondies

Nonstick spray or oil, for the pan

1¼ cups (165 g) all-purpose flour

½ teaspoon baking powder

¼ teaspoon baking soda

¼ teaspoon kosher salt

½ cup (1 stick / 113 g) unsalted butter

⅔ cup packed (134 g) dark brown sugar

2 large eggs

1 teaspoon pure vanilla extract

Preheat the oven to 325°F (165°C) with a rack in the center of the oven. Lightly spray or oil a 13-by-9-inch (33-by-23-cm) pan, line it with a strip of parchment paper, extending it over two sides, then lightly spray or oil the parchment paper.

Whisk together the flour, baking powder, baking soda, and salt in a small bowl; set aside.

Melt the butter in a medium saucepan over medium heat, then cook several minutes longer, swirling occasionally, until it smells nutty and turns a deep golden brown, taking care not to let it burn. Immediately remove the butter from the heat and pour it into a heatproof bowl. Use a whisk to stir in the brown sugar, then let cool until no longer hot to the touch, about 5 minutes. Whisk in the eggs one at a time, mixing well after each addition. Stir in the vanilla. Stir in the flour mixture just until no white streaks remain.

Spread the batter evenly into the prepared pan, leveling it with a moistened offset spatula. Bake until the edges just begin to color slightly and a toothpick inserted near the center finds some moist crumbs clinging to it, about 20 minutes, rotating the pan front to back halfway through baking. Cool the blondies in the pan for 10 minutes, then use the parchment paper to lift and transfer the blondies on the parchment to a wire rack to cool completely.

SANDWICH!

Form sandwiches using Method #4 on page 19. Once firmly frozen, cut the sandwiches into 3 strips the long way and 4 strips the short way to make 12 sandwiches. Alternatively, form the sandwiches using ice cream sandwich molds following Method #2.

TAKE IT EASY

Use store-bought blondies and dulce de leche or caramel ice cream. Or swirl store-bought or homemade dulce de leche (page 158) into softened vanilla ice cream.

DRESS IT UP

Roll the sides of the sandwiches in chopped toasted walnuts. Or dip the sandwiches into a bowl of warm dulce de leche as you eat them.

Vietnamese Breakfast

Vietnamese Coffee
Ice Cream on Parisian
Cocoa Macarons

When the French colonized Vietnam in the late nineteenth century, they began planting coffee there. As fresh milk and refrigeration were hard to come by, they tamed the drink's bitter edge with sweetened condensed milk. Old habits die hard, and the Vietnamese have retained their canned milk habit despite the availability of fresh. As a nod to those French roots, I've sandwiched Vietnamese coffee ice cream between petite Parisian-style chocolate macarons.

Vietnamese Coffee Ice Cream GF

⅓ cup (24 g) dark-roasted coffee beans, regular or decaffeinated

2 cups (480 ml) whole milk

5 teaspoons tapioca starch

¼ teaspoon kosher salt

¾ cup (225 g) sweetened condensed milk (not evaporated milk)

2 tablespoons strained yogurt (page 27), labne, or plain Greek yogurt, at room temperature

1 teaspoon pure vanilla extract

¼ teaspoon espresso-grind coffee

Crack the coffee beans by putting them on a flat surface and pressing the bottom of a cast-iron skillet over them. (Alternatively, pulse them briefly in a coffee grinder.)

Heat the milk in a medium saucepan until it begins to bubble around the edges; do not boil. Remove from the heat, stir in the coffee beans, and let steep for 30 minutes.

Strain the milk and return it to the saucepan; discard the beans. Put a few tablespoons of the infused milk in a medium bowl and whisk in the tapioca and salt until no lumps remain. Add the tapioca mixture to the saucepan with the milk and heat the mixture over medium-high heat, stirring with a heatproof spatula, until it begins to steam and slightly bubble at the edges. Adjust to a simmer and cook, stirring constantly, until the mixture thickens to the consistency of a cream sauce, about 2 minutes longer; do not fully boil.

In the same bowl, whisk the sweetened condensed milk, yogurt, vanilla, and ground coffee until smooth. Add a small amount of the thickened milk, stir until smooth, then stir in the remaining thickened milk.

Set the bowl over a larger bowl of ice and water, and stir occasionally until the mixture is cool, taking care not to slosh water into the bowl. Cover and refrigerate until very cold, at least 2 hours. Transfer the bowl to the freezer for the last half hour before spinning it.

Freeze the mixture in an ice cream maker according to the manufacturer's directions. When it is ready, transfer to a chilled container and freeze until firm, at least 4 hours or overnight.

Parisian Cocoa Macarons GF DF

1½ cups (200 g) almond meal (see Note)

2½ cups (300 g) powdered sugar

1 tablespoon unsweetened cocoa powder, natural or Dutch-processed

4 large egg whites, at room temperature

¼ cup (50 g) granulated sugar

½ teaspoon cream of tartar

Line two baking sheets with parchment paper or silicone baking mats.

Process the almond meal and powdered sugar in a food processor to make a fine powder, about 1 minute. Add the cocoa powder and pulse to combine.

Beat the egg whites and cream of tartar in a stand mixer with the whisk attachment (or with a handheld electric mixer) on low speed until the whites are frothy. With the mixer running, add the granulated sugar, about a tablespoon at a time, pausing for a few seconds between additions, until it is all incorporated. Scrape down the bowl with a spatula, then raise the speed to high and beat until the whites form firm peaks that hold their shape and curl just slightly when you stop and invert the beater.

Use a spatula to fold one-third of the almonds into the whites, then fold in the remaining almonds. You will lose quite a bit of the whites' air as you fold, which is necessary for the cookie's texture.

Using half of the macaron mixture, fill a pastry bag fitted with a ½-inch (1½-cm) round tip (or a zipper-top bag with a ½-inch / 1½-cm opening cut in one corner) and pipe 1-inch (2½-cm) circles on one baking sheet, evenly spaced, to make 24 circles. Repeat to make 24 circles on the second sheet. Lift and drop the baking sheets on the counter once or twice from about

1 inch (2½ cm) above to settle the macarons, then let them stand at room temperature until the tops are dry to the touch, about 60 minutes.

Preheat the oven to 325°F (165°C) with racks in the upper and lower thirds of the oven.

Bake the macarons until they are completely dry and just starting to color on the bottoms, about 15 minutes, rotating the pans top to bottom and front to back halfway through baking.

Transfer the sheets to a wire rack until the macarons are completely cooled. If you cannot easily lift them from the paper, use a small offset spatula to loosen them.

SANDWICH!

Form sandwiches using Method #1 on page 18, using a generous tablespoon of ice cream per sandwich. These sandwiches are best enjoyed up to 48 hours after filling them. For longer storage, freeze the ice cream and cookies separately and form the sandwiches shortly before serving them.

NOTE: To grind your own almond meal, process whole almonds in a food processor until they are nearly as fine as flour, adding the powdered sugar after the almonds are partially ground. It's a good practice to keep nuts fresh by storing them in the freezer, and grinding them cold helps keep them from turning to nut butter.

TAKE IT EASY

Use store-bought coffee ice cream and bakery macarons or other chocolate cookies.

DRESS IT UP

Roll the edges in Almond Crack (page 163), or fold Mocha Ripple (page 156) and Almond Crack into the ice cream to make mocha almond fudge.

Everything Is Rosie

Rosewater Ice Cream on
Pistachio-Cardamom Sandies

MAKES 10 SANDWICHES

This sandwich combines exotic Middle Eastern and Indian flavors in an alluring sandwich. Found in the ethnic foods aisle of grocery stores, or in Middle Eastern and Indian markets, rosewater provides classic rose fragrance (see Sources and Resources, page 168). Brands vary considerably in their intensity, so sample the mixture and add more if you wish, bit by bit, until you find it pleasingly but not overwhelmingly rosy. Keep in mind that you'll want the flavor to come through when sandwiched with the cookies.

Rosewater Ice Cream GF

2 cups (480 ml) whole milk

⅔ cup (134 g) granulated sugar

2 tablespoons tapioca starch

2 tablespoons inverted sugar syrup (page 27), golden syrup, or light agave nectar

¼ teaspoon kosher salt

1½ cups (360 ml) heavy cream

2 tablespoons strained yogurt (page 27), labne, or plain Greek yogurt, at room temperature

1 teaspoon rosewater, or to taste (see Note)

Whisk ½ cup (120 ml) of the milk with the sugar, tapioca, syrup, and salt in a medium saucepan until no lumps remain. Whisk in the remaining 1½ cups (360 ml) milk.

Heat the mixture over medium-high heat, stirring with a heatproof spatula, until it begins to steam and slightly bubble at the edges. Adjust to a simmer and cook, stirring constantly, until the mixture thickens to the consistency of a cream sauce, about 90 seconds longer; do not fully boil. Remove from the heat.

Stir the cream and yogurt together in a small bowl until smooth, then stir them into the milk mixture. Add the rosewater. Taste and add more rosewater, if desired, a little at a time, to achieve a subtle but certain rose flavor.

Transfer the mixture to a metal bowl set over a larger bowl of ice and water. Stir occasionally until the mixture is cool, taking care not to slosh water into the bowl. Cover and refrigerate until very cold, at least 2 hours. Transfer the bowl to the freezer for the last half hour before spinning it.

While the ice cream spins, line a 9-inch (23-cm) square baking pan with waxed paper and place it in the freezer. When the ice cream is ready, spread it evenly into the prepared pan, cover with plastic wrap, pressing it directly against the surface, and freeze until firm, at least 6 hours or overnight.

Pistachio-Cardamom Sandies

½ cup (70 g) shelled pistachios, lightly toasted and cooled (see page 25)

¼ cup (50 g) granulated sugar

½ teaspoon (5 to 6) green cardamom pods, or ½ teaspoon ground cardamom

½ cup (1 stick / 113 g) unsalted butter, softened

1 cup (132 g) all-purpose flour

¼ teaspoon kosher salt

2 tablespoons turbinado or other coarse sugar, for rolling

Process the nuts, granulated sugar, and cardamom in a food processor to the texture of coarse meal but not so far as to make a paste. It's fine if there are a few larger pieces, but they should be generally fine. Add the butter and process until smooth and creamy, about 1 minute, stopping to scrape down the bowl as needed. Add the flour and salt, pulsing several times to form a dough.

Transfer the dough to a lightly floured surface and bring it together into a mass, then shape it into a 5¼-inch (13-cm) log.

Lay a sheet of plastic wrap on a flat surface and sprinkle it with the turbinado sugar. Roll the log across the sugar, pressing it into the sugar to coat it evenly. Wrap the log tightly, pressing the ends against a flat surface to flatten them, keeping the log at its 5¼-inch (13-cm) length. Refrigerate until very firm, about 2 hours. (Alternatively, roll out the dough between two floured sheets of plastic wrap to ¼ inch / 6 mm thick and cut with 2½-inch / 6-cm cookie cutters; sprinkle the tops with turbinado sugar.)

About 20 minutes before baking, preheat the oven to 350°F (175°C) with racks in the upper and lower thirds of the oven. Line two baking sheets with parchment paper or silicone baking mats.

Unwrap the log and use a sharp knife to shave ⅛ inch (3 mm) off of each end (press together into a cookie and bake as a snack),

then cut the log into twenty ¼-inch-thick (6-mm) slices. Evenly space the cookies on the prepared baking sheets and bake until the cookies begin to color around the edges, about 13 minutes, rotating the pans top to bottom and front to back halfway through baking. Slide the cookies on their liners to a wire rack to cool completely.

SANDWICH!

Form sandwiches using Method #3 on page 19, using a 2½-inch (6-cm) cutter to cut out 10 rounds of the ice cream, gathering scraps to form the last round or two, if needed. Alternatively, form sandwiches using Method #1.

NOTE: To flavor the ice cream with rose petals or rose geranium instead of rosewater, warm the milk to a simmer and add the rinsed petals of 6 large, fragrant, unsprayed roses or a dozen rose geranium leaves. Let infuse off the heat for 20 minutes (start checking after 5 minutes with the rose geranium), then strain out and discard the petals or leaves and use the flavored milk to prepare the ice cream, adding rosewater at the end if desired to intensify the flavor.

TAKE IT EASY

Use store-bought sugar cookies. Stir rosewater to taste into softened vanilla ice cream.

DRESS IT UP

Roll the sides of the sandwiches in chopped toasted pistachios—lightly salted, if you wish— or sugared rose petals.

Everything Is Rosie (pages 102–103)

Tea Time

Jasmine Ice Cream on
Almond Tea Cakes

MAKES
12
SANDWICHES

Delicate jasmine ice cream sits between two delectably chewy almond cookies adapted from the blog She Simmers (shesimmers.com), written by Leela, a Thai woman living in the Midwest. For the best flavor, use a good-quality jasmine tea, preferably the type hand-rolled into small pearl-like balls, called Jasmine Pearl tea or Jasmine Dragon Phoenix Pearls. This cookie works well with ice cream sandwich molds.

Jasmine Ice Cream GF

2 cups (480 ml) whole milk

2 tablespoons jasmine pearl tea

⅔ cup (134 g) granulated sugar

2 tablespoons tapioca starch

¼ teaspoon kosher salt

2 tablespoons inverted sugar syrup (page 27), golden syrup, or agave nectar

1½ cups (360 ml) heavy cream

Heat the milk in a medium saucepan until it steams and bubbles at the edges; do not boil. Off the heat, stir in the tea and let stand, sampling the infusion every 5 minutes or so until the milk has a pronounced jasmine flavor but is not at all bitter, 10 to 15 minutes.

Whisk the sugar, tapioca, and salt in a medium bowl to evenly combine them. Strain the infused milk into the sugar mixture, adding about ½ cup (120 ml) at first and stirring to make a smooth paste, then adding the rest; discard the tea.

Return the mixture to the saucepan and stir in the syrup. Heat the mixture over medium-high heat, stirring with a heatproof spatula, until it begins to steam and slightly bubble at the edges. Adjust to a simmer and cook, stirring constantly, until the mixture thickens to the consistency of a cream sauce, about 90 seconds longer; do not fully boil. Remove from the heat, transfer the mixture back to the bowl, and stir in the cream.

Set the bowl over a larger bowl of ice and water, and stir occasionally until the mixture is cool, taking care not to slosh water into the bowl. Cover and refrigerate until very cold, at least 2 hours.

Transfer the bowl to the freezer for the last half hour before spinning it.

Freeze the mixture in an ice cream maker according to the manufacturer's directions. While the ice cream spins, line a 13-by-9-inch (33-by-23-cm) baking pan with waxed paper and place it in the freezer. When the ice cream is ready, spread it evenly into the prepared pan, cover with plastic wrap, pressing it directly against the surface, and freeze until firm, at least 4 hours or overnight.

Almond Tea Cakes GF DF

2 cups (300 g) blanched almonds

¾ cup packed (150 g) light brown sugar

1 large egg

1 large egg yolk

2 tablespoons mild-flavored honey or golden syrup

1 teaspoon baking soda

½ teaspoon kosher salt

2 tablespoons turbinado or other coarse sugar, for sprinkling

Preheat the oven to 350°F (175°C) with racks in the upper and lower thirds of the oven. Line two baking sheets with parchment paper or silicone baking mats.

Process the nuts in a food processor until they are very fine, with some just beginning to form a paste around the edges. Scrape the bowl, then add the brown sugar, egg and yolk, honey, baking soda, and salt. Process until a sticky dough forms, scraping the bowl as needed.

Run a 1-tablespoon scoop under the tap and shake off the excess water, then use it to form 24 portions of the mixture, wetting the scoop as needed. Roll the dough between your palms to form smooth balls, then space them evenly on the prepared sheets. Sprinkle the tops with turbinado sugar and use a flat-bottom drinking glass or your fingers to flatten them into rounds

that are ¼-inch (6-mm) thick and about 1½ inch / 4 cm in diameter. (Moisten the glass bottom or spray it with nonstick pan spray if the dough sticks.) Leave at least an inch (2½ cm) of space all around the cookies for spreading.

Bake until the cookies are puffed, cracked, and light golden all over, 10 to 12 minutes, rotating the pans top to bottom and front to back halfway through baking. The tops will be soft.

Let the cookies cool completely on the sheets.

SANDWICH!

Form sandwiches using Method #3 on page 19, using a 2½-inch (6-cm) cutter to cut out 12 rounds of the ice cream, gathering scraps to form the last round or two, if needed. Alternatively, form the sandwiches using ice cream sandwich molds following Method #2.

TAKE IT EASY

Use store-bought soft almond cookies or other cookies. Store-bought green tea ice cream, which is typically flavored with matcha rather than jasmine, also pairs well with the cookies.

DRESS IT UP

The delicate ice cream is easily over-whelmed—this one is best left alone.

My Thai

Kaffir Lime and Lemongrass
Sorbet on Five-Spice Cookies

MAKES
12
SANDWICHES

This sandwich captures Thai flavorings in a coconut-based sorbet. Lemongrass is available in well-stocked produce markets. Look for fresh or frozen kaffir lime leaves in markets where Asian ingredients are sold. In a pinch, approximate the leaf's exotic herbal-citrus flavor by substituting the outer zest from one common (Persian) lime, cut in wide strips, and half of a bay leaf. Galangal root is in the ginger family, and has a similar, though more distinctively floral, slightly pungent flavor.

The five-spice powder in the cookies balances and complements the ice cream. Szechuan peppercorn is a traditional ingredient in five-spice powder that (sadly) is often missing. It adds to the mystique, so if you have some on hand or can easily find it, do include it.

Kaffir Lime and Lemongrass Sorbet GF DF

6-inch (15-cm) length of fresh lemongrass, white portion only

6 kaffir lime leaves

2 (⅛-inch / 3-mm thick) slices of galangal or ginger root (optional)

2 cans (about 13.5 ounces / 400 ml each) coconut milk

½ cup packed (100 g) light brown sugar

2 tablespoons tapioca starch

¼ teaspoon kosher salt

¼ cup (60 ml) inverted sugar syrup (page 27), golden syrup, or mild-flavored honey

2 tablespoons fresh lime juice

My Thai (left) and Tea Time (right, recipe on page 104)

Lay the lemongrass on a flat surface and whack it with the bottom of a heavy knife handle to bruise it all along the length of the stalk. Drop it into a medium saucepan. Tear the lime leaves into a few pieces to release their essence and drop them into the pan, along with the galangal, if using. Pour the coconut milk over the aromatics, then heat over medium heat until the milk steams and bubbles at the edges; do not boil. Stir, then let the milk steep off the heat for about 20 minutes, tasting it periodically until it is well flavored. Strain the mixture into a bowl, pressing on the aromatics; discard the solids.

In the saucepan (no need to wash it), whisk the brown sugar, tapioca, and salt to combine them. Whisk in the sugar syrup and a bit of the infused coconut milk to make a smooth paste.

Add the rest of the infused milk while whisking until it is all combined. Heat the mixture over medium-high heat, stirring with a heatproof spatula, until it begins to steam and slightly bubble at the edges. Adjust to a simmer and cook, stirring constantly, until the mixture thickens to the consistency of a cream sauce, about 2 minutes longer; do not fully boil. Remove from the heat and transfer the mixture back to the bowl.

Set the bowl over a larger bowl of ice and water, and stir occasionally until the mixture is cool, taking care not to slosh water into the bowl. Stir in the lime juice. Cover and refrigerate until very cold, at least 2 hours. Transfer the bowl to the freezer for the last half hour before spinning it.

Freeze the mixture in an ice cream maker according to the manufacturer's directions. While the sorbet spins, line a 13-by-9-inch (33-by-23-cm) baking pan with waxed paper and place it in the freezer. When the sorbet is ready, spread it evenly into the prepared pan, cover with plastic wrap, pressing it directly against the surface, and freeze until firm, at least 4 hours or overnight.

Five-Spice Cookies GF DF

1 recipe Almond Tea Cakes (page 105)

1 teaspoon five-spice powder, or ¾ teaspoon five-spice plus ¼ teaspoon ground Szechuan peppercorns

Follow the recipe instructions for the Almond Tea Cakes on page 105, adding the five-spice powder along with the salt.

SANDWICH!

Form sandwiches using Method #3 on page 19, using a 2½-inch (6-cm) cutter to cut out 12 rounds of the ice cream, gathering scraps to form the last round or two, if needed. Alternatively, form the sandwiches using ice cream sandwich molds following Method #2.

TAKE IT EASY

Use store-bought soft almond cookies or five-spice cookies.

DRESS IT UP

Roll the sides of the sandwiches in chopped toasted almonds or pistachios, or in toasted coconut.

Spicy Date

Date Sorbet on Brown Sugar–
Walnut Bars

MAKES
16
SANDWICHES

Many consider the plump, dark, wrinkled Medjool the finest of all dates. Grown on large date palms primarily in southeastern California and southwestern Arizona, this ancient fruit of Moroccan royalty may be found year-round. The California Medjool Date Council explains that this is the sole variety sold only fresh or frozen, never dried.

Where I live, vendors drive north to sell the dates at farmers' markets, where one small sample convinces a good number of passers-by to take home a pint. If you have fallen prey, I have a Moroccan-inspired idea for you. It just might win you a date.

Date Sorbet GF DF

3 cups (720 ml) unsweetened coconut milk beverage, such as Coconut Dream or So Delicious

1 cup packed (300 g) pitted Medjool dates (about 20 dates), coarsely chopped

⅓ cup packed (67 g) brown sugar

2 tablespoons mild-flavored honey, golden syrup, or agave nectar

¼ teaspoon ground ginger

¼ teaspoon ground cinnamon

¼ teaspoon ground cardamom

¼ teaspoon ground allspice

¼ teaspoon kosher salt

Pour the coconut milk into a medium saucepan and add the dates, brown sugar, and honey. Stir over medium-low heat until the dates are soft and falling apart, about 10 minutes. Use an immersion blender or standard blender to blend the mixture until it is completely smooth.

Strain the mixture through a regular-mesh strainer into a medium bowl, pressing to push as much of the puree through as possible; discard the solids. Stir in the spices and salt.

Set the bowl over a larger bowl of ice and water. Stir occasionally until the mixture is cool, taking care not to slosh water into the bowl. Cover and refrigerate until very cold, at least 2 hours. Transfer the bowl to the freezer for the last half hour before spinning it.

Freeze the mixture in an ice cream maker according to the manufacturer's directions. When it is ready, transfer the ice cream to a chilled container, cover, and freeze until firm but still spreadable, about 4 hours.

Brown Sugar–Walnut Bars

1 cup (132 g) all-purpose flour

½ teaspoon ground cinnamon

½ teaspoon baking soda

¼ teaspoon kosher salt

½ cup (1 stick / 113 g) unsalted butter, plus more for the pan

½ cup packed (100 g) dark brown sugar

1 large egg

½ teaspoon pure vanilla extract

½ cup (50 g) rolled oats

½ cup (60 g) toasted walnuts, chopped medium-fine (see page 25)

Preheat the oven to 350°F (175°C) with racks in the upper and lower thirds of the oven. Butter two 8-inch (20-cm) square pans. Line the pans with parchment paper, fitting it snugly into the pan so that the ends extend up two sides. Butter the parchment. (Alternatively, use one 13-by-9-inch / 33-by-23-cm pan, which will result in slightly smaller, thicker bars.)

Whisk the flour, cinnamon, baking soda, and salt in a small bowl; set aside.

Stir the butter and brown sugar in a small saucepan over medium heat just until the butter melts. Transfer the mixture to a medium bowl and stir in the egg and vanilla, mixing well. Stir in the flour mixture until only a few white streaks remain, then stir in the oats and walnuts.

Divide the batter evenly between the two pans, spreading it in each pan and leveling it with an offset spatula. Bake until puffed, with the edges just beginning to color, about 12 minutes, rotating the pans top to bottom and front to back halfway through baking. A toothpick inserted near the center should find some moist crumbs clinging to it. Cool the bars in the pan for 10 minutes, then use the parchment paper to lift and transfer the bars on the parchment to a wire rack to cool completely.

SANDWICH!

Form sandwiches using Method #4 on page 19. Once firmly frozen, cut the sandwiches into 4 strips in each direction to form 16 bars.

TAKE IT EASY

Substitute soft ginger cookies for the brown sugar walnut bars.

DRESS IT UP

Roll the sides of the sandwiches in chopped toasted walnuts or Maple-Buttered Pecans (page 162).

6

Scoop and Serve

Some of the most exciting textural contrasts come from sandwiches made *à la minute*, using whatever you have on hand to contain a melting scoop of ice cream. Here, we venture from traditional sandwich holders to the eccentric, with buttered toast, brioche rolls, croissants, and hot dog buns. These sandwiches are ready for instant gratification, made either one at a time or for a crowd. You'll find more suggestions for offbeat sandwich holders in recipe sidebars throughout the book and in Sandwich It Your Way! (page 166).

Milk and Cookies (page 114)

Milk and Cookies

Milk Gelato on Warm Chocolate Chip Cookies

In Italy, milk is the quintessential gelato flavor that lets pure dairy shine, without even a dribble of vanilla. It's the perfect companion for that quintessential *American* treat, the fresh-from-the-oven, warm chocolate chip cookie. Could anything be more comforting?

I've used whole wheat flour in the cookies for its nutty flavor and oat flour for chewy texture. Right out of the oven, the cookies are the perfect pairing for this ice cream, but they also retain their soft-chewy texture when frozen. Because milk is the main source of its flavor, it's worth seeking out good, fresh, preferably local and organic milk for this one. If you can find milk from Jersey cows at your local farmers' market, this is a fine way to use it.

Milk Gelato GF

2 cups (480 ml) whole milk

⅓ cup (67 g) granulated sugar

2 tablespoons inverted sugar syrup (page 27), golden syrup, or light agave nectar

2 tablespoons tapioca starch

¼ teaspoon kosher salt

1 cup (240 ml) heavy cream

Whisk ½ cup (120 ml) of the milk with the sugar, syrup, tapioca, and salt in a medium saucepan until no lumps remain. Stir in the remaining 1½ cups (360 ml) milk and the cream. Heat the mixture over medium-high heat, stirring with a heatproof spatula, until it begins to steam and slightly bubble at the edges. Adjust to a simmer and cook, stirring constantly, until the mixture thickens to the consistency of a cream sauce, about 3 minutes longer; do not fully boil.

Transfer the mixture to a metal bowl set over a larger bowl of ice and water. Stir occasionally until the mixture is cool, taking care not to slosh water into the bowl. Cover and refrigerate until very cold, at least 2 hours. Transfer the bowl to the freezer for the last half hour before spinning it.

Freeze the mixture in an ice cream maker according to the manufacturer's directions. When it is ready, transfer the gelato to a chilled container, cover, and freeze until firm, at least 4 hours or overnight.

Chocolate Chip Cookies

1 cup (132 g) whole wheat pastry flour or all-purpose flour

¼ cup (33 g) oat flour, baby oats, or additional whole wheat pastry or all-purpose flour

½ teaspoon baking powder

¼ teaspoon kosher salt

½ cup (1 stick / 113 g) unsalted butter

⅓ cup packed (67 g) light brown sugar

¼ cup (50 g) granulated sugar

1 tablespoon inverted sugar syrup (page 27) or golden syrup

1 tablespoon neutral vegetable oil

1 large egg

½ teaspoon pure vanilla extract

1 cup (200 g) bittersweet (dark) chocolate chips

Whisk together the pastry flour, oat flour, baking powder, and salt in a bowl; set aside.

Melt the butter with the brown sugar in a small saucepan, stirring to dissolve the sugar. Transfer to a medium bowl and whisk in the granulated sugar, syrup, and oil until well mixed. Whisk in the egg and vanilla until well blended, then mix in the flour mixture until only a few streaks of flour remain. When the mixture is completely cool, use a spatula to mix in the chocolate chips with the last few folds of flour. Refrigerate the dough while the oven preheats, or cover and refrigerate for up to 24 hours.

About 20 minutes before baking, preheat the oven to 325°F (165°C) with racks in the upper and lower thirds of the oven. Line two baking sheets with parchment paper or silicone baking mats.

Pinch off tablespoon-size pieces of dough to make 24 approximately equal pieces, spacing them evenly on the prepared baking sheets. Roll the dough between your palms to form balls and return them to sheets. Press the cookies with your palms to flatten them to 2 inches (5 cm) in diameter (about ¼ inch / 6 mm thick).

Bake until the cookies have lost their sheen, 10 to 11 minutes, rotating the pans top to bottom and front to back halfway through baking. The cookies will be quite soft but will firm up as they cool. Let the cookies cool on the pans for 5 minutes, then transfer the cookies on their liners to a wire rack until they are barely warm.

SANDWICH!

Form the sandwiches using Method #1 on page 18, using freshly baked cookies and serving them immediately after filling.

TAKE IT EASY

Use bakery-style or slice-and-bake chocolate chip cookies and store-bought vanilla ice cream.

DRESS IT UP

The neutral flavor of the ice cream is the perfect invitation to run wild with mix-ins. Fold in any of the swirls or ripples, chopped nuts or nut brittle, or chopped candies (see page 167 for ideas). Or serve the sandwiches with gently warmed Chocolate Shell (page 165) or Salty Caramel Swirl (page 156) for dipping.

PB&J

MAKES 12 SANDWICHES

This is my go-to sandwich when I am jonesing for one and there are none stashed away in the freezer. Sometimes I hope *not* to find a sandwich there, just so I can make this one, which delights with warm toast, cool ice cream, and the reassuring flavors of childhood. With ice cream awaiting in your freezer, a sandwich need never be more than a toaster away.

I make these up one at a time when the mood strikes. If you're hosting a child's sleep-over party or have family in town for the holidays, make all twelve at once for an easy and memorable breakfast or midnight snack.

Peanut butter is personal: Choose creamy for a smooth ice cream or chunky for more texture. In either case, look for a natural-style peanut butter made from only peanuts (salt optional), with no sweeteners or gums. I prefer a mild honey such as clover or orange blossom for this ice cream.

Peanut Butter Ice Cream GF

2 cups (480 ml) whole milk

½ cup (100 g) granulated sugar

¼ cup (84 g) mild-flavored honey

2 tablespoons tapioca starch

¼ teaspoon kosher salt

⅔ cup (160 g) natural peanut butter

1 cup (240 ml) heavy cream

½ teaspoon pure vanilla extract

Whisk ½ cup (120 ml) of the milk with the sugar, honey, tapioca, and salt in a medium saucepan until no lumps remain. Stir in the remaining 1½ cups (360 ml) milk. Heat the mixture over medium-high heat, stirring with a heatproof spatula, until it begins to steam and slightly bubble at the edges. Adjust to a simmer and cook, stirring constantly, until the mixture thickens to the consistency of a cream sauce, 2 to 3 minutes longer; do not fully boil.

Off the heat, add the peanut butter, give it a minute or two to soften, then stir until smooth and well blended. Stir in the cream and vanilla.

Transfer the mixture to a metal bowl set over a larger bowl of ice and water. Stir occasionally until the mixture is cool, taking care not to slosh water into the bowl. Cover and refrigerate until very cold, at least 2 hours. Transfer the bowl to the freezer for the last half hour before spinning it.

Freeze the mixture in an ice cream maker according to the manufacturer's directions. When it is ready, transfer the ice cream to a chilled container, cover, and freeze until firm, at least 4 hours or overnight.

Toast and Berry "Jam"

1 to 12 slices good-quality sandwich bread, such as challah, bakery white, or honey whole wheat

Unsalted butter, for spreading on the toast (optional)

1 to 12 tablespoons Berry Ribbon (page 159), or berry jam or fruit spread

SANDWICH!

For each sandwich, toast 1 slice of bread until it is medium dark. Trim the crusts and butter the bread if you wish. Cut the slice in half, either crosswise or diagonally, as you would a sandwich. Spread 1 tablespoon of Berry Ribbon on one toast half. Scoop and spread ¼ cup (60 ml) slightly softened ice cream across the other half. Sandwich the two together and enjoy while the toast is warm.

TAKE IT EASY

For each sandwich, mix 2 teaspoons of peanut butter with 1 teaspoon of honey and swirl into a scoop of softened vanilla ice cream. Use your favorite jam, jelly, or fruit spread in place of the Berry Ribbon.

DRESS IT UP

For extra peanut punch, press the sides of the sandwich in Honey-Roasted Peanut Brittle (page 162).

Sicilian Breakfast

Pistachio Gelato on a Brioche Bun

MAKES 12 SANDWICHES

When I learned while traveling in Sicily that a common breakfast there is made of gelato tucked inside a brioche roll, I nearly phoned home for my belongings and relocated on the spot. The soft, eggy roll makes a fine companion to the creamy-chewy ice cream, soaking up the melting treat rather than leaving it to drip from the bottom of a cone. *Magnifico!*

The Sicilian town of Bronte grows some of the world's most prized pistachios, so I've chosen that iconic Sicilian flavor to pair with the brioche, enhanced by almonds, which also grow on the island. If you can find Sicilian pistachios and almonds, you are in for a truly exceptional treat.

Pistachio Gelato GF

1 cup (135 g) raw shelled pistachios

½ cup (70 g) almonds, blanched or skin-on

2 tablespoons golden syrup, inverted sugar syrup (page 27), or agave nectar

¼ teaspoon kosher salt

2½ cups (600 ml) whole milk

½ cup plus 2 tablespoons (125 g) granulated sugar

2 tablespoons tapioca starch

Process the pistachios and almonds in a food processor until they become a nut paste, occasionally scraping down the bowl. Be patient—it takes time. Mix in the golden syrup and salt. Leave the paste in the bowl.

Whisk ½ cup (120 ml) of the milk with the sugar and tapioca in a medium saucepan until no lumps remain. Whisk in the remaining 2 cups (480 ml) milk. Heat the mixture over medium-high heat, stirring with a heatproof spatula, until it begins to steam and slightly bubble at the edges. Adjust to a simmer and cook, stirring constantly, until the mixture thickens to the consistency of a cream sauce, about 3 minutes longer; do not fully boil.

Carefully scrape the hot thickened milk into the food processor bowl; process briefly to combine. Carefully transfer the hot mixture to a metal bowl set over a larger bowl of ice and water. Stir occasionally until the mixture is cool, taking care not to slosh water into the bowl. Cover and refrigerate until very cold, at least 2 hours. Transfer the bowl to the freezer for the last half hour before spinning it.

(continued on page 122)

Freeze the mixture in an ice cream maker according to the manufacturer's directions. When it is ready, transfer the gelato to a chilled container, cover, and freeze until firm, at least 4 hours or overnight.

Brioche Buns

⅓ cup (80 ml) whole milk, plus 1 tablespoon for glazing

2 teaspoons active dry yeast

2 cups (264 g) all-purpose flour

1 tablespoon granulated sugar, plus 2 teaspoons for glazing

1 teaspoon kosher salt

2 large eggs, at room temperature, plus 1 egg for glazing

½ cup (1 stick / 113 g) unsalted butter, cool but not ice cold, cut into ½-inch (1½-cm) cubes

Neutral vegetable oil, for coating the dough

Gently heat the ⅓ cup (80 ml) milk in a small saucepan over medium-low heat until it is warm but not too hot to easily touch (about 105°F / 41°C). Sprinkle the yeast over the milk and stir to dissolve it. Set aside.

Mix together the flour, 1 tablespoon of the sugar, and the salt in a stand mixer with the dough hook. On medium-low speed, add 2 eggs, then add the dissolved yeast until the dough comes together in a ball. Mix at medium speed until the dough is smooth and elastic, 8 to 10 minutes, scraping the bowl as needed. It is ready when you can stretch a piece of dough between your fingers almost thin enough to see through without it tearing. Add the butter, several pieces at a time, waiting until each addition is fully incorporated before adding the next. It will take about 8 minutes.

Gather the dough in your hands to form a neat ball, lightly rub the surface with oil, and set it back in the mixer bowl. Cover the bowl with plastic wrap and let stand at room temperature until doubled in volume, 60 to 90 minutes.

Line a baking sheet with parchment paper or a silicone baking mat. Turn the dough out onto a flat surface and press it gently to release the trapped gas. Cut the dough into 12 pieces. Use a cupped hand to roll each piece on a flat surface to form a ball. Space the rolls evenly on the baking sheet, seam side down, and press them gently to slightly flatten. Cover the rolls with damp dish towels or plastic wrap and let rise at room temperature until doubled in volume, 45 to 60 minutes.

During the last half hour of rising, preheat the oven to 375°F (190°C) with a rack in the center. Whisk the remaining egg with 1 tablespoon of milk in a small bowl to make a glaze.

Brush the roll tops with the glaze and sprinkle them lightly with the remaining 2 teaspoons sugar. Bake until golden, 18 to 20 minutes, rotating the pan front to back halfway through baking.

Cool the rolls on the pan for about 5 minutes, then transfer them to a wire rack to cool completely, or sandwich them while slightly warm. Store unused rolls in an airtight container for up to 2 days.

SANDWICH!

Split the rolls, leaving them hinged on one side. Pull out (and enjoy) some of the soft insides from the top and bottom of the roll to form a well. Tuck a scoop or two of slightly softened gelato inside, press gently to close, and serve immediately.

TAKE IT EASY

Use good-quality store-bought brioche rolls and store-bought gelato.

DRESS IT UP

Spread Chocolate-Hazelnut Spread, Fudge Ripple, or Berry Ribbon (pages 156 to 161) on the bun before filling.

S'mores

Fudge Ripple Ice Cream on Graham Crackers with Toasted Marshmallows

MAKES 12 SANDWICHES

This sandwich takes the favorite campfire treat to the freezer, but keeps the pyrotechnics: You'll get to torch the marshmallow before enclosing it and the ice cream between graham crackers. A tunnel of fudge in the ice cream pays homage to the chocolate bars in the original. While marshmallows may seem fussy to make, they are not difficult and are the *sine qua non* of s'mores.

I cannot get enough of these graham crackers, for which I thank Smitten Kitchen, Martha Stewart, and Nancy Silverton (via Heidi Swanson) for their online guidance. Made either with graham or whole wheat flour, this adapted version has the familiar taste of store-bought graham crackers, but is more tender and less sweet—my new go-to snacking cookie.

Fudge Ripple Ice Cream GF

1 recipe Vanilla Ice Cream (page 30)

1 recipe Fudge Ripple (page 156)

Prepare the ice cream following the recipe instructions. While the ice cream spins, line a 13-by-9-inch (33-by-23-cm) baking pan with plastic wrap and place it in the freezer. When the ice cream is ready, spread it evenly into the prepared pan, swirling it with the Fudge Ripple (see page 156). Cover with plastic wrap, pressing it directly against the ice cream, and freeze until firm, at least 6 hours or overnight.

Graham Crackers

¾ cup (100 g) all-purpose flour

¾ cup (100 g) graham flour or whole wheat flour

⅓ cup packed (67 g) brown sugar

½ teaspoon kosher salt

¼ teaspoon baking soda

2 tablespoons milk, whole or 2%

2 tablespoons mild-flavored honey

2 teaspoons pure vanilla extract

6 tablespoons (85 g) unsalted butter, cold, cut into ½-inch (1½-cm) cubes

1 tablespoon turbinado or granulated sugar, for sprinkling

Pulse the all-purpose and graham flours, brown sugar, salt, and baking soda in a food processor. Add the milk, honey, and vanilla; pulse several times to combine. Scatter the butter over the top and pulse until the mixture clumps and holds together when you press it between your fingers.

Transfer the dough to a piece of plastic wrap and use your hands to bring it together into a ball. Flatten the dough into a rough rectangle, wrap, and refrigerate until firm, about 1 hour.

Preheat the oven to 350°F with a rack in the center of the oven. Line a baking sheet with parchment paper.

Roll the dough between two pieces of plastic wrap into a 14-by-10-inch (35½-by-25-cm) rectangle, then trim it to 13 by 9 inches (33 by 23 cm). Remove the top plastic and flip the dough onto the prepared baking sheet.

Peel away the plastic and use a straight or fluted cutter (a pizza cutter works well) to cut the dough into 4 strips the long way and 6 the short way to make 24 rectangles, approximately 2 by 2¼ inches (5 by 5½ cm). (It's helpful to measure and mark each of the strips at both ends and use a ruler as a guide when you cut them.) Sprinkle the tops with the turbinado sugar, then use a fork to prick each cracker in two or three neat rows.

Bake the crackers until they are puffed and a shade darker golden, about 14 minutes, rotating the pan front to back halfway through baking. Let the cookies cool on the pan for 5 minutes. Retrace the cut lines with the same cutter, then carefully transfer the individual cookies to a wire rack to cool completely.

Toasted Marshmallows GF DF

12 Vanilla-Scented Marshmallows (page 163) or store-bought marshmallows

SANDWICH!

Form sandwiches using Method #3 on page 19, using a knife or cutter to cut the ice cream into 12 approximately 2-by-2¼-inch (5-by-5½-cm) rectangles to match the graham crackers. (Pack the remaining ice cream for another use.) Place ice cream rectangles on 12 cookies and freeze them open-faced in an airtight container until ready to serve. Store the tops in a separate airtight container at room temperature, ready to be placed at serving time.

To serve, place one marshmallow per sandwich on a parchment-lined baking sheet and toast, either by waving a kitchen torch over them until they are dark brown all over, or placing the sheet under the broiler, watching carefully until the marshmallows are deeply toasted. Working swiftly, use a small offset spatula to place each torched marshmallow on an ice cream—topped cracker, then cover with a second cracker. Press down gently and serve immediately.

TAKE IT EASY

Use store-bought graham crackers and fudge swirl ice cream. For the best texture and flavor, seek out handmade marshmallows in ice cream and candy shops rather than commercially produced ones.

DRESS IT UP

Use vanilla ice cream in place of the fudge ripple and dip the sandwiches in Chocolate Shell (page 165), allowing the shell to harden for just 5 minutes before serving. Or coat the graham crackers in Chocolate Shell, letting it dry before forming the sandwiches.

Apricot Croissan'wich

Apricot Sorbet
on a Croissant

I am crazy for apricots, and my favorite variety is the Royal Blenheim. These tiny fruits are packed with concentrated flavor and a fleshy-juicy texture, almost as if they're on their way to becoming dried fruits. My backyard tree puts out a pathetic crop thanks to our cool Bay Area climate and shade from neighboring trees. The squirrels and birds steal most of them before they're ripe enough to pick. Fortunately, for a few weeks in June and July, they show up at my neighborhood farmers' market. It takes only a little sugar, gentle cooking, and a bit of good-quality fruit preserves to amplify the fruit's essence.

To showcase the fruit's delicate flavor, I've tucked it into a buttery croissant. This makes it seem reasonable to enjoy the sandwich at my favorite time: for brunch, after returning from the Sunday morning farmers' market.

Apricot Sorbet GF DF

1½ pounds (680 g) ripe apricots, pitted and halved

½ cup (100 g) granulated sugar

¼ cup (80 ml) inverted sugar syrup (page 27), golden syrup, or agave nectar

2 tablespoons apricot preserves

¼ teaspoon kosher salt

1 tablespoon fresh lemon juice

Put the apricots, sugar, syrup, preserves, salt, and 1 cup of water in a medium saucepan. Bring to a simmer over medium heat, stirring to dissolve the sugar. Simmer gently until the apricots are tender, about 5 minutes.

Puree the mixture using an immersion blender, or in a standard blender, until smooth. Strain the puree through a fine- or regular-mesh strainer into a bowl, pressing on the solids to extract as much flavor as possible; discard the solids. Stir in the lemon juice.

Cover and refrigerate until very cold, at least 2 hours. Transfer the bowl to the freezer for the last half hour before spinning it.

Freeze the sorbet in an ice cream maker according to the manufacturer's directions. When it is ready, transfer the sorbet to a chilled container. Cover and freeze until firm, at least 4 hours or overnight.

Croissants

1 to 9 croissants, fresh from a good bakery

SANDWICH!

For each sandwich, split a croissant with a serrated knife from front to back, leaving it hinged at the back. Warm the croissant in a toaster oven or on a baking sheet in a preheated 400°F (205°C) oven for a few minutes, just until it is warm and toasty. Pull out (and enjoy) some of the soft insides from both the top and bottom of the croissant to form a well.

Scoop about 1/3 cup (80 ml) of sorbet (depending on the size of the croissant), spreading it to fill the croissant. Close and serve immediately.

TAKE IT EASY

Substitute any store-bought sorbet or ice cream, especially fruit-based flavors.

DRESS IT UP

Spread Berry Ribbon (page 159) or another ribbon or spread on the croissant before filling, depending on the sorbet or ice cream flavor. Sprinkle the ice cream with chopped toasted nuts.

Banana Split

Assorted Ice Creams and
Toppings on a Hot Dog Bun
with Caramelized Banana

MAKES
6
SANDWICHES

If gelato tucked into a brioche bun makes for the perfect solitary walk-about Sicilian breakfast, this version is the one for a gang. Part sandwich, part sundae, it's a great way to use up bits of leftover ice cream and sauces, all while maintaining a semblance of health (bananas! berry sauce! fruit and nut garnish!). I've even used soft honey–whole wheat buns in place of the brioche and they perfectly soaked up all the melty ice cream and sauces. (Nevertheless, a plate beneath is advisable with this one.)

For a banana split party, line up the buns, sugar-crusted bananas, ice cream with small scoops, bowls of sauce, and any additional toppings, and let everyone make their own. For a children's birthday party, cut the buns in half crosswise and serve one half with a banana quarter to make 12 minis.

Assorted Ice Creams and Toppings

3 or more flavors of ice cream, enough to make 18 small scoops in total (1 to 2 tablespoons per scoop)

3 or more sauces, such as Salty Caramel Swirl (page 156), Fudge Ripple (page 156), and Berry Ribbon (page 159)

Any additional toppings you desire, such as fresh berries, chopped toasted nuts, marshmallows, whipped cream, or candied cherries

Hot Dog Buns

1 recipe Brioche Buns (page 122), dough not formed or baked

Follow the recipe for Brioche Buns (page 122), cutting the dough into 6 pieces rather than 12. Shape each dough piece into an elongated, 4-inch-long (10-cm) bun. Rise, glaze, and bake according to the recipe directions. As they are larger, these will take 20 to 25 minutes to bake. Let the buns cool completely.

Caramelized Bananas GF DF

3 bananas, peeled and split lengthwise

2 to 4 tablespoons granulated sugar

Lay out the bananas cut-side up on a flat flameproof surface and sprinkle each half evenly with 1 to 2 teaspoons of sugar. Holding a kitchen torch 1 to 2 inches (2½ to 5 cm) from the surface, move the flame slowly and steadily over the bananas until the sugar melts and then browns, 1 to 2 minutes. Alternatively, broil the sugared bananas on a baking sheet as close as possible to the heating element, watching closely until the sugar is melted and golden brown, 2 minutes or longer, depending on your broiler.

SANDWICH!

Split and open the buns, leaving them hinged on one side. Remove some of the soft insides from both sides of the bun to form a well.

For each sandwich, place a bun on a plate and lay a caramelized banana against the top half of the open bun. Place 3 small scoops of slightly softened ice cream on the bottom half, up against the seam. Top each scoop with a spoonful of sauce, warmed if desired, and any additional toppings you wish. Press gently to close the bun, and serve immediately.

TAKE IT EASY

Use soft, good-quality bakery or store-bought hot dog buns. Use store-bought ice cream or gelato, any flavors you wish, and store-bought toppings and sauces.

DRESS IT UP

Visit Sandwich It Your Way! (page 166) and go to town with the optional embellishments.

Chapter 7

Holidays and Special Occasions

Wow your family and friends with these extravagant treats, all dressed up for the holidays. For parties and events, use your favorite cookie cutters to cut the ice cream and sandwich holders into matching shapes for easy assembly, then embellish them by wrapping a strip of parchment around the center and securing it with twine or a ribbon.

Be Mine (page 134)

Be Mine

What could be more fitting for Valentine's Day than luscious pink raspberry ice cream sandwiched between heart-shaped chocolate cookies? Perhaps a little bling in the form of shiny pink sugar? Now *that* spells L-O-V-E.

This cookie works quite sweetly with the Tovolo heart-shaped ice cream sandwich mold (page 170), following the manufacturer's directions, or using a heart-shaped cutter to form the sandwiches. Larger molds will yield fewer sandwiches.

Raspberry Swirl Ice Cream GF

2 cups (260 g) raspberries, fresh or frozen (thawed)

¾ cup (150 g) granulated sugar

2 tablespoons Framboise or raspberry wine (optional)

1 tablespoon fresh lemon juice

¼ teaspoon kosher salt

1 cup (240 ml) whole milk

2 tablespoons tapioca starch

1 cup (240 ml) heavy cream

1 recipe Berry Ribbon (page 159), using raspberries, regular or Smashed Framboise version

Stir the berries, sugar, Framboise, if using, lemon juice, and salt in a medium nonreactive saucepan over medium heat until the fruit has collapsed and the liquid is syrupy, about 5 minutes. Press the mixture through a regular-mesh strainer into a bowl; discard the solids. (Wear an apron—the berries stain!)

Stir ¼ cup (60 ml) of the milk with the tapioca starch in the same saucepan until no lumps remain, then stir in the remaining ¾ cup (180 ml) milk and the strained berry mixture. Heat the mixture over medium-high heat, stirring with a heatproof spatula, until it begins to steam and slightly bubble at the edges. Adjust to a simmer and cook, stirring constantly, until the mixture thickens to the consistency of a cream sauce, about 90 seconds longer; do not fully boil. Remove from the heat, transfer the mixture back to the bowl, and stir in the cream.

Set the bowl over a larger bowl of ice and water, and stir occasionally until the mixture is cool, taking care not to slosh water into the bowl. Cover and refrigerate until very cold, at least 2 hours. Transfer the bowl to the freezer for the last half hour before spinning it.

Freeze the mixture in an ice cream maker according to the manufacturer's directions. While the ice cream spins, line a 13-by-9-inch (33-by-23-cm) baking pan with waxed paper and place it in the freezer. When the ice cream is ready, spread it evenly into the pan, drizzling it with the Berry Ribbon. Cover with plastic wrap, pressing it directly against the surface, and freeze until firm, at least 6 hours or overnight.

Chocolate Sweethearts

1 cup (132 g) all-purpose flour

⅓ cup (33 g) unsweetened Dutch-processed cocoa powder

¼ teaspoon kosher salt

½ cup (1 stick / 113 g) unsalted butter, softened

¾ cup (150 g) granulated sugar

1 large egg

1 teaspoon pure vanilla extract

2 tablespoons pink or other coarse sugar, for sprinkling

Preheat the oven to 350°F (175°C) with a rack in the center of the oven. Line a rimless baking sheet with parchment paper. Whisk together the flour, cocoa powder, and salt in a small bowl; set aside.

Mix the butter and sugar in a stand mixer using the paddle attachment on medium-high speed until fluffy, about 5 minutes. Scrape down the bowl with a spatula, then mix in the egg and vanilla until well combined. Add the flour mixture just until no white streaks remain. (Alternatively, use a handheld electric mixer, or mix by hand with a wooden spoon in a bowl.)

Use a dampened small offset spatula to spread the thick, sticky batter evenly on the parchment paper to cover as large an area as you can, aiming for 15 by 12 inches (38 by 30½ cm). Sprinkle the dough evenly with the coarse sugar.

Bake just until the surface is no longer shiny, about 10 minutes. Slide the cookie on its parch-ment onto a flat surface. While the cookie is still warm and soft, use a heart-shaped (or other) cookie cutter or mold to cut out as many cookies as you can, aiming for 24, cutting each right up against the last to fit as many cookies as possible. Transfer the cookies to a wire rack to cool completely.

SANDWICH!

Form sandwiches using Method #3 on page 19, using the same cutter you used for the cookies to cut up to 12 hearts (depending on cutter size) from the ice cream, gathering scraps to form the last heart or two, if needed. Alternatively, form sandwiches using Method #2, using a heart-shaped ice cream sandwich mold or a 2-inch-tall (5-cm) heart-shaped cutter.

TAKE IT EASY

Use store-bought chocolate cookies, heart-shaped or otherwise, cutting the ice cream accordingly. Swirl Berry Ribbon (page 159) into softened raspberry or vanilla ice cream.

DRESS IT UP

For that special someone, adding a second swirl of Fudge Ripple (page 156) is well worth the small additional effort. Or dip the sandwiches into Chocolate Shell (page 165) to cover half of each sandwich, letting it set for 15 minutes in the freezer.

Easter Rabbi

Coconut Sorbet on
Chocolate-Coconut Macaroons

MAKES
12
SANDWICHES

Pinned to our refrigerator last spring was a picture of a chocolate rabbi, the caption reading: "No, not a chocolate rabbi, I said *rabbit*!" Loaded with coconut and free of grains and dairy, this sandwich built on chewy macaroons celebrates Passover, Easter, or whatever spring holiday you favor.

Coconut Sorbet GF DF

1½ cups (360 ml) unsweetened coconut beverage, such as Coconut Dream or So Delicious

⅔ cup (134 g) granulated sugar

2 tablespoons inverted sugar syrup (page 27), golden syrup, or light agave nectar

5 teaspoons tapioca starch

¼ teaspoon kosher salt

1 can (about 13.5 ounces/400 ml) unsweetened coconut milk (not light), such as Chaokoh or Mae Ploy brands

⅔ cup (67 g) unsweetened finely shredded coconut

Whisk ½ cup (120 ml) of the coconut beverage with the sugar, syrup, tapioca, and salt in a medium saucepan until no lumps remain. Stir in the remaining 1 cup (240 ml) coconut beverage.

Heat the mixture over medium-high heat, stirring with a heatproof spatula, until it begins to steam and slightly bubble at the edges. Adjust to a simmer and cook, stirring constantly, until the mixture thickens to the consistency of a cream sauce, 1 to 2 minutes longer; do not fully boil. Transfer the mixture to a metal bowl and stir in the canned coconut milk and shredded coconut.

Set the bowl over a larger bowl of ice and water, and stir occasionally until the mixture is cool, taking care not to slosh water into the bowl. Cover and refrigerate until very cold, at least 2 hours. Transfer the bowl to the freezer for the last half hour before spinning it. (Strain the mixture through a fine-mesh strainer before spinning for smooth sorbet; leave the coconut in for a chewier texture.)

Freeze in an ice cream maker according to the manufacturer's directions. When it is ready, transfer to a chilled container and freeze until firm, at least 6 hours or overnight.

Chocolate-Coconut Macaroons GF DF

¾ cup (113 g) blanched almonds

½ cup (100 g) granulated sugar

2 large egg whites

¼ teaspoon kosher salt

2 ounces (57 g) unsweetened chocolate, melted and cooled to room temperature

½ teaspoon pure vanilla extract, or a pinch of ground vanilla bean

1 cup (100 g) unsweetened finely shredded coconut

Preheat the oven to 325°F (165°C) with racks in the upper and lower thirds of the oven. Line two baking sheets with parchment paper or silicone baking mats.

Process the almonds with the sugar in a food processor to make a fine meal, about 1 minute, pulsing or scraping the bowl occasionally to bring up the nuts that have fallen to the bottom. Add the egg whites and salt; process to combine. Add the chocolate and vanilla and process again just to combine. Remove the bowl from the processor and stir in the coconut by hand to combine everything evenly.

Drop the batter by the heaping teaspoon in 12 evenly spaced mounds on each of the two prepared baking sheets, making 24 in total, with plenty of space surrounding them on all sides. Spread the mounds with a small offset spatula, or press them with moistened fingers, to make 2½-inch (6-cm) rounds.

Bake until the macaroons are dry to the touch, about 10 minutes, rotating the pans top to bottom and front to back halfway through baking. Let the cookies cool on the sheets for 5 minutes, then transfer them to wire racks to cool completely.

SANDWICH!

Form sandwiches using Method #1 on page 18, using ¼ cup (60 ml) of sorbet per sandwich.

TAKE IT EASY

Use store-bought macaroons and coconut sorbet or ice cream.

DRESS IT UP

Roll the sides in toasted shredded coconut or chopped toasted nuts. For Easter, roll the sides in miniature, multi-colored jelly beans.

Cinco de Mayo

MAKES 24 SANDWICHES

These miniature spicy chocolate sandwiches celebrate chocolate's Mayan ancestry, with cinnamon, ancho chile powder, and a hint of cayenne. The grated chocolate simulates the grainy texture of Mexican chocolate; a small Microplane shaver is the perfect tool for this, but you can use any grater or finely chop the chocolate. With the smaller amount of cayenne the ice cream is gently spicy; increase it from there as you wish keeping in mind that the heat will build as the ice cream matures. As Mexican chocolate is often made with almonds, these Parisian-style almond macarons are the perfect holder.

Spicy Mexican Chocolate Ice Cream GF

2 cups (480 ml) whole milk

½ cup (100 g) granulated sugar

¼ cup (25 g) good-quality unsweetened Dutch-processed cocoa

3 tablespoons tapioca starch

2 tablespoons golden syrup, agave nectar, or inverted sugar syrup (page 27)

1 teaspoon ground cinnamon

½ teaspoon ancho chile powder

⅛ to ¼ teaspoon cayenne pepper

¼ teaspoon kosher salt

1 cup (240 ml) heavy cream

1 teaspoon pure vanilla extract

3 ounces (85 g) grated or finely chopped bittersweet (60 to 70 percent) chocolate

Whisk ½ cup (120 ml) of the milk with the sugar, cocoa powder, tapioca, golden syrup, cinnamon, chile powder, cayenne, and salt in a medium saucepan until the cocoa is fully moistened. Stir in the remaining 1½ cups (360 ml) milk.

Heat the mixture over medium-high heat, stirring with a heatproof spatula, until it begins to steam and slightly bubble at the edges. Adjust to a simmer and cook, stirring constantly, until the mixture thickens to the consistency of a cream sauce, about 2 minutes longer; do not fully boil.

Transfer the mixture to a metal bowl and stir in the cream and vanilla. Set the bowl over a larger bowl of ice and water, and stir occasionally until the mixture is cool, taking care not to slosh water into the bowl. Cover and refrigerate until very cold, at least 2 hours. Transfer the bowl to the freezer for the last half hour before spinning it.

Freeze in an ice cream maker according to the manufacturer's directions, adding the grated

chocolate during the last minute of spinning. When it is ready, transfer to a chilled container and freeze until firm, at least 8 hours or overnight.

Cinnamon Macarons GF DF

1½ cups (200 g) almond meal
(see Note on page 98)

2½ cups (300 g) powdered sugar

¼ teaspoon ground cinnamon

4 large egg whites, at room temperature

½ teaspoon cream of tartar

¼ cup (50 g) granulated sugar

Line two baking sheets with parchment paper or silicone baking mats.

Process the almond meal and powdered sugar in a food processor to make a fine powder, about 1 minute. Add the cinnamon and pulse to combine.

Beat the egg whites and cream of tartar in a stand mixer with the whisk attachment (or with a handheld electric mixer), starting on low speed, until the whites are frothy. With the mixer running, add the granulated sugar, about 1 tablespoon at a time, pausing for a few seconds between additions, until it is all incorporated. Scrape down the bowl with a spatula, then raise the speed to high and beat until the whites form firm peaks that hold their shape and curl just slightly when you stop and invert the beater.

Use a spatula to fold one-third of the almonds into the whites, then fold in the remaining almonds. You will lose quite a bit of the whites' air as you fold, which is necessary for the cookie's texture.

Using half of the macaron mixture, fill a pastry bag fitted with a ½-inch (1½-cm) round tip (or a zipper-top bag with a ½-inch / 1½-cm opening cut in one corner), and pipe 1-inch (2½-cm) circles on one baking sheet, evenly spaced, to make 24 circles. Repeat to make 24 circles on the second sheet. Lift and drop the baking

sheets on the counter once or twice from about 1 inch (2½ cm) above to settle the macarons, then let them stand at room temperature until the tops are dry to the touch, about 60 minutes.

Preheat the oven to 325°F (165°C) with racks in the upper and lower thirds of the oven.

Bake the macarons until they are completely dry and just starting to color on the bottoms, about 15 minutes, rotating the pans top to bottom and front to back halfway through baking.

Transfer the sheets to a wire rack until the macarons are completely cooled. If you cannot easily lift the macarons from the paper, use a small offset spatula to loosen them.

SANDWICH!

Form sandwiches using Method #1 on page 18, using a generous 1 tablespoon of ice cream per sandwich. Avoid squeezing—just scoop and top with a second macaron. These sandwiches are best enjoyed up to 48 hours after filling them. For longer storage, freeze the ice cream and macarons separately and form the sandwiches shortly before serving them.

TAKE IT EASY

Use store-bought macarons or meringue cookies. Stir the ice cream spices and grated chocolate into softened chocolate ice cream.

DRESS IT UP

Roll the sides of the sandwiches in cacao nibs, grated Mexican chocolate, mini chocolate chips, or chopped toasted almonds.

4th of July

White Corn and Red Raspberry Ice
Cream on Cornmeal Cookies

MAKES 12 SANDWICHES

This sandwich has you covered for all of the major barbecue occasions from Memorial Day to Labor Day. Use blue cornmeal (see Bob's Red Mill in Sources and Resources, page 168) to complete the 4th of July theme colors, or use regular cornmeal and garnish the sandwich platter with a handful of blueberries. The flavor combination was inspired by the very first recipe I developed for my book *Farmers' Market Desserts*: a cornmeal cake studded with fresh corn kernels and berries. The alluring combination of sweet, earthy corn and sweet-tart berries has remained a favorite, and is complemented here by a pleasing crunch from cornmeal in the cookies.

White Corn and Red Raspberry Ice Cream GF

2 large ears white corn, husks and silks removed

1½ cups (360 ml) whole milk

⅓ cup (67 g) granulated sugar

1 tablespoon mild-flavored honey, golden syrup, or light agave nectar

1 tablespoon tapioca starch

⅛ teaspoon kosher salt

¾ cup (180 ml) heavy cream

2 tablespoons strained yogurt (page 27), labne, or plain Greek yogurt, at room temperature

1 recipe Berry Ribbon (page 159), made with raspberries

Cut the kernels from the corn with a sharp knife and break the cobs in half. Put the milk into a medium-size heavy saucepan and add the corn kernels. With the back of the knife, scrape any remaining corn from the cobs into the pot before dropping in the cobs. Bring the milk to a simmer, turn off the heat, and set aside to infuse for 20 minutes.

Remove the corn cobs, scraping any milk clinging to them back into the pot before discarding them. Transfer the corn-milk to a blender and puree until nearly smooth. Pour the mixture through a fine-mesh strainer back into the saucepan, pressing on the solids to extract as much of the milk as you can; discard the solids.

To the corn-milk in the saucepan, add the sugar, honey, tapioca, and salt. Stir until no lumps of tapioca remain. Heat the mixture over medium-high heat, stirring with a heatproof spatula, until

it begins to steam and slightly bubble at the edges. Adjust to a simmer and cook, stirring constantly, until the mixture thickens to the consistency of a cream sauce, about 90 seconds longer; do not fully boil. Transfer the mixture to a metal bowl.

Stir the cream and yogurt together until smooth, then whisk into the ice cream mixture. Set the bowl over a larger bowl of ice and water and stir occasionally until the mixture is cool, taking care not to slosh water into the bowl. Cover and refrigerate until very cold, at least 2 hours. Transfer the bowl to the freezer for the last half hour before spinning it.

Freeze the mixture in an ice cream maker according to the manufacturer's directions. When it is ready, transfer the ice cream to a chilled container, swirling it with the Berry Ribbon as you pack the ice cream into the container (see page 156). Cover and freeze until firm, at least 4 hours or overnight.

Cornmeal Cookies

1⅓ cups (176 g) all-purpose flour

⅔ cup (100 g) fine or medium stone-ground cornmeal, blue or yellow

⅓ cup (67 g) granulated sugar

½ teaspoon baking powder

½ teaspoon kosher salt

½ cup (1 stick / 113 g) unsalted butter, cold, cut into ½-inch (1½-cm) cubes

1 large egg

1 tablespoon turbinado or other coarse sugar

Preheat the oven to 350°F (175°C) with racks in the upper and lower thirds of the oven. Line two baking sheets with parchment paper or silicone baking mats.

Pulse the flour, cornmeal, sugar, baking powder, and salt in a food processor to combine them. Scatter the butter over the top, then pulse until the mixture has the texture of coarse meal.

Add the egg and process until the dough balls up around the processor blade.

Pinch off tablespoon-size pieces of dough to make 24 approximately equal pieces, spacing them evenly on the prepared baking sheets. Roll the dough between your palms to form balls, dunk one side of each ball in turbinado sugar, and space them evenly on the baking sheets, sugar-side up. Press the cookies with the bottom of a glass or your hands to flatten them to 2½-inch (6-cm) diameter. (Moisten the glass bottom or spray it with nonstick pan spray if the dough sticks.) Alternatively, roll the dough between two pieces of plastic wrap and cut with cookie cutters.

Bake until the cookies begin to color around the edges only, 13 to 15 minutes, rotating the pans top to bottom and front to back halfway through baking. Let the cookies cool on the pans for 5 minutes, then transfer the cookies on their liners to a wire rack until they are completely cooled.

SANDWICH!

Form sandwiches using Method #1 on page 18, using ¼ cup (60 ml) of ice cream per sandwich.

TAKE IT EASY

Substitute store-bought cornmeal or almond cookies. Stir Berry Ribbon (page 159) and kernels cut from an ear of sweet, fresh corn into softened vanilla ice cream.

DRESS IT UP

Roll the sides of the sandwiches in corn kernels cut from an ear of sweet, tender corn, or in finely chopped toasted almonds. Or serve the sandwiches with a bowl of Smashed Framboise Ribbon (page 160) for dipping.

Giving Thanks

Boozy Pumpkin-Pecan Ice
Cream on Maple Leaf Cookies

MAKES
12
SANDWICHES

These pretty sandwiches combine two of my favorite reasons for giving thanks: pumpkin pie and the Maple Leaf, a cocktail made with bourbon and maple syrup. The crisp, spicy cookies are cut into leaf shapes in keeping with the autumnal theme. The true reason for thanks: the swarm of friends and family who will clamor for this distinctive holiday dessert.

You'll need a 2½- to 3-inch (6- to 7½-cm) maple leaf cookie cutter, or another festive autumn cutter. Look for maple sugar in specialty and natural food stores, or order it online from King Arthur Flour (see Sources and Resources, page 168).

Boozy Pumpkin-Pecan Ice Cream GF

1 cup (245 g) pureed pumpkin, fresh or canned

1 cup (240 ml) whole milk

1 cup (240 ml) heavy cream

⅔ cup (160 ml) pure maple syrup, preferably Grade B or A dark amber

3 tablespoons bourbon, brandy, or rum

2 tablespoons tapioca starch

½ teaspoon kosher salt

¼ teaspoon ground cinnamon

¼ teaspoon ground ginger

2 tablespoons crème fraîche, sour cream, or strained yogurt (page 27), at room temperature

½ teaspoon pure vanilla extract

1 recipe Maple-Buttered Pecans (page 162)

Process the pumpkin, milk, cream, maple syrup, bourbon, tapioca, salt, cinnamon, and ginger in a blender until smooth. Transfer the mixture to a medium saucepan and heat over medium-high heat, stirring with a heatproof spatula, until it begins to steam and slightly bubble at the edges. Adjust to a simmer and cook, stirring constantly, until the mixture thickens to the consistency of a cream sauce, about 3 minutes longer; do not fully boil.

Whisk the crème fraîche and vanilla in a medium bowl until smooth. Add about ½ cup (120 ml) of the thickened pumpkin mixture, stirring until smooth, then stir in the rest of the pumpkin mixture.

Set the bowl over a larger bowl of ice and water. Stir occasionally until the mixture is cool, taking care not to slosh water into the bowl. Cover and refrigerate until very cold, at least 2 hours. Transfer the bowl to the freezer for the last half hour before spinning it.

Freeze the mixture in an ice cream maker according to the manufacturer's directions, adding the pecans during the last minute of spinning. While the ice cream spins, line a 13-by-9-inch (33-by-23-cm) baking pan with waxed paper and place it in the freezer. When the ice cream is ready, spread it evenly into the prepared pan, cover with plastic wrap, pressing it directly against the surface, and freeze until firm, at least 6 hours or overnight.

Maple Leaf Cookies

1 cup (132 g) all-purpose flour

1 teaspoon baking powder

½ teaspoon ground cinnamon

¼ teaspoon ground ginger

¼ teaspoon ground allspice

½ teaspoon kosher salt

½ cup (1 stick / 113 g) unsalted butter, softened

¾ cup (150 g) pure maple sugar or granulated sugar

2 tablespoons pure maple, turbinado, or coarse sugar, for sprinkling

Preheat the oven to 325°F (165°C) with racks in the upper and lower thirds of the oven. Line two baking sheets with parchment paper or silicone baking mats.

Whisk together the flour, baking powder, cinnamon, ginger, allspice, and salt in a small bowl. Set aside.

Beat the butter and ¾ cup (150 g) maple sugar in a medium bowl with a handheld electric mixer until creamy. (Alternatively, use a wooden spoon.) Mix in the flour mixture just until well combined. (If using a mixer, it may be easier to finish the mixing by hand.)

Roll out the dough between two pieces of plastic wrap (lightly floured, if needed) to ¼ inch (6 mm) thick. Remove the top plastic and use a leaf-shaped cutter to cut out 24 cookies, gathering and re-rolling the scraps up to two more times to make all of the cookies. Transfer the cookies as you cut them to the prepared baking sheets. Sprinkle the cookies with the remaining 2 tablespoons maple sugar.

Bake until the cookies are a shade darker golden than when they went in, about 14 minutes, rotating the pans top to bottom and front to back halfway through baking. Let the cookies cool for 5 minutes on the sheets, then slide the cookies on the parchment to wire racks to cool completely.

SANDWICH!

Form sandwiches using Method #3 on page 19, using the same cutter used to cut the cookies to cut out 12 shapes from the ice cream, gathering scraps to form the last one or two, if needed. Alternatively, form sandwiches using Method #1.

TAKE IT EASY

Use store-bought maple or sugar cookies. Process pumpkin puree in a food processor until smooth and mix into softened vanilla ice cream; add pie spices and chopped pecans if you wish.

DRESS IT UP

Fold half of the maple-buttered pecans into the ice cream and save the rest for rolling the sides of the sandwiches. Or serve the ice cream between warm, crispy-ridged waffles and drizzle with maple syrup.

Winter Holidays

A friend who is crazy for mint chocolate chip ice cream requested this one year for his birthday. It has since made regular appearances, not only on his birthday, but also to brighten the winter holidays, a job it does especially well when dressed up with crushed candy canes. The brownies are the same as the ones used in the Wake-up Call sandwich (page 43). Espresso is optional this time, but surprisingly, it complements the mint beautifully.

Mint Chocolate Chip Ice Cream GF

2 cups (480 ml) whole milk

⅓ cup (67 g) granulated sugar

2 tablespoons golden syrup, inverted sugar syrup (page 27), or light agave nectar

2 tablespoons tapioca starch

¼ teaspoon kosher salt

1 cup (240 ml) heavy cream

6 to 8 drops pure peppermint oil (see Note, page 150)

½ cup (100 g) bittersweet (60 to 70 percent) chocolate, chopped or chips

1 tablespoon neutral vegetable oil or coconut oil

Whisk ½ cup (120 ml) of the milk with the sugar, golden syrup, tapioca, and salt in a medium saucepan until no lumps remain. Stir in the remaining 1½ cups (360 ml) milk and the cream. Heat the mixture over medium-high heat, stirring with a heatproof spatula, until it begins to steam and slightly bubble at the edges. Adjust to a simmer and cook, stirring constantly, until the mixture thickens to the consistency of a cream sauce, about 3 minutes longer; do not fully boil.

Transfer the mixture to a metal bowl set over a larger bowl of ice and water. Stir occasionally until the mixture is cool, taking care not to slosh water into the bowl. Stir in 4 to 5 drops of peppermint oil, to taste, then cover and refrigerate until very cold, at least 2 hours. Transfer the bowl to the freezer for the last half hour before spinning it.

Freeze the mixture in an ice cream maker according to the manufacturer's directions. While the mixture spins, melt the chocolate and vegetable oil in the microwave or in a small saucepan over low heat until you can stir it smooth. Stir in 2 to 3 drops of peppermint oil, to taste. Let cool

to room temperature, keeping it fluid.

With the machine running, drizzle in the melted chocolate during the last minute of spinning. (Alternatively, drizzle the chocolate over the ice cream as you transfer it to the container, folding it in with a spatula or ice cream paddle to break it up as you go.) Transfer the ice cream to a chilled container, cover, and freeze until firm but still spreadable, about 4 hours.

Fudge Brownies

1 recipe Espresso Fudge Brownies (page 46), espresso optional, baked in two 8-inch (20-cm) square pans

SANDWICH!

Form sandwiches using Method #4 on page 19. Once firmly frozen, cut the filled brownie into 3 strips in one direction and 2 in the other, then cut each bar diagonally in two to form 12 triangular sandwiches. Alternatively, form the sandwiches using ice cream sandwich molds following Method #2.

NOTE: While I love infusing ice cream with mint from my garden, I must admit that nothing conveys clean, cool minty flavor more clearly than pure peppermint oil, which is far more concentrated (and delicious) than peppermint extract. I buy the 1-dram bottles of LorAnn brand (see Sources and Resources, page 168) which, despite their tiny size, seem to last forever. In a pinch, substitute 1 teaspoon of pure peppermint extract in the ice cream, or more to taste, and add a few drops to the melted chocolate for making the chips.

TAKE IT EASY

Use a brownie mix, adding 1 teaspoon instant espresso granules, if desired. Bake the brownies in two pans until still slightly moist at the center, about 5 minutes less than specified on the box. Use store-bought mint chocolate chip ice cream, or mix 4 to 5 drops of peppermint oil and mini chocolate chips into softened vanilla or chocolate ice cream.

DRESS IT UP

Roll the sides of the sandwiches in crushed candy canes. Serve with minty hot cocoa topped with Vanilla-Scented Marshmallows (page 163).

Auld Lang Syne

Champagne-Caramel Swirl Ice Cream on Vanilla Cookies in a Black-and-White Tuxedo

This sandwich is dressed and ready for the New Year's Eve ball, the year's last indulgence before the merry-making ends and the resolution-making begins. Champagne ice cream might seem decadent enough, but the swirl takes the Champagne's delicate toasty flavor into a frenzied tango of salt and caramel. You'll need only a good glug of sparkling wine for the ice cream, so cork it up and save the rest for celebrating on New Year's Eve or Day.

A champagne toast to Robert Burns, the Scot who penned the timeless lyric celebrating times past and yet to come!

Champagne-Caramel Swirl Ice Cream GF

1½ cups (360 ml) whole milk

⅓ cup (67 g) granulated sugar

2 tablespoons golden syrup, inverted sugar syrup (page 27), or agave nectar

2 tablespoons tapioca starch

¼ teaspoon kosher salt

1 cup (240 ml) heavy cream

⅓ cup (80 ml) Champagne or sparkling wine, such as Cava or Prosecco

½ teaspoon pure vanilla extract

¾ cup (180 ml) Salty Caramel Swirl (page 156)

Whisk ½ cup (120 ml) of the milk with the sugar, golden syrup, tapioca, and salt in a medium saucepan until no lumps remain. Stir in the remaining 1 cup (240 ml) milk and the cream. Heat the mixture over medium-high heat, stirring with a heatproof spatula, until it begins to steam and slightly bubble at the edges. Adjust to a simmer and cook, stirring constantly, until the mixture thickens to the consistency of a cream sauce, about 3 minutes longer; do not fully boil.

Transfer the mixture to a metal bowl set over a larger bowl of ice and water. Stir occasionally until the mixture is cool, taking care not to slosh water into the bowl. Cover and refrigerate until very cold, at least 2 hours. Transfer the bowl to the freezer for the last half hour before spinning it.

Stir the Champagne and vanilla into the ice cream mixture, then freeze in an ice cream maker according to the manufacturer's directions. When it is ready, transfer the ice cream to a chilled container, swirling it with the Salty Caramel Swirl as you pack the ice cream into the container (see page 156). Cover and freeze until firm, at least 6 hours or overnight.

Vanilla Cookies

1 cup (132 g) all-purpose flour

1 teaspoon baking powder

¼ teaspoon kosher salt

½ cup (1 stick / 113 g) unsalted butter, softened

¾ cup (150 g) granulated sugar

½ teaspoon pure vanilla extract

Preheat the oven to 300°F (150°C) with racks in the upper and lower thirds of the oven. Line two rimless baking sheets with parchment paper or silicone baking mats.

Whisk together the flour, baking powder, and salt in a small bowl. Set aside.

Beat the butter and sugar in a medium bowl with a handheld electric mixer until creamy. (Alternatively, use a wooden spoon.) Add the vanilla. Mix in the flour mixture just until well combined. (If using a mixer, it may be easier to finish the mixing by hand.)

Divide the dough into 24 pieces, rolling each between your palms into a smooth ball, and space them evenly on the baking sheets. Use a flat-bottom drinking glass to flatten each ball to a 2½-inch (6-cm) round. (Moisten the glass bottom or spray it with nonstick pan spray if the dough sticks.)

Bake until the cookies are firm but not yet colored, about 14 minutes, rotating the pans top to bottom and front to back halfway through baking. Slide the cookies on their liners to a flat surface and, for the dressiest sandwiches, while they are still warm and soft, use a 2½-inch (6-cm) cutter to trim them into perfect rounds. Transfer the cookies to wire racks to cool completely.

Black-and-White Tuxedo GF DF

1 recipe Chocolate Shell (page 165), made with 12 ounces (340 g) white chocolate and 3 table-spoons neutral vegetable oil or coconut oil

1 recipe Chocolate Shell (page 165), made with 12 ounces (340 g) extra bittersweet (64 to 72 percent) chocolate and 2 tablespoons neutral vegetable oil or coconut oil

SANDWICH!

Form sandwiches using Method #1 on page 18, neatly smoothing the edges. Freeze until firm, at least 2 hours, before dipping.

Dip the firmly frozen sandwiches in the white chocolate to coat them halfway, following the instructions for Chocolate Shell on page 165. Transfer the sandwiches to a baking sheet in the freezer until the chocolate sets, 10 to 15 minutes. Repeat to dip the second half of each sandwich in dark chocolate. Return to the freezer until set, at least 15 minutes.

TAKE IT EASY

Use store-bought sugar cookies or bakery black and white cookies. Use store-bought caramel-swirl ice cream, or swirl Salty Caramel Swirl (page 156) into softened vanilla ice cream.

DRESS IT UP

This one is already well dressed—no further embellishments needed.

Extra Credit: Swirls, Mix-ins, Roll-'ems, and Coatings

Looking to give your favorite ice cream sandwich that special twist? These add-ons will dress up your sandwiches, taking them to the stratosphere with your own signature style.

Swirls, Ripples, Ribbons, and Dippers

Swirl your ice cream by folding a fruit, fudge, or caramel sauce into just-processed or softened ice cream. One-half to 1 cup of swirl is about right for a quart or a liter of ice cream.

It's best to add ribbons and swirls by hand as you pack your ice cream from the machine into a chilled container in order to keep the ice cream and swirl distinct. Drizzle some of the swirl, ripple, or ribbon into the bottom of the container, dollop in about one-third of the ice cream, and continue drizzling and adding ice cream until you've used everything up, ending with a drizzle over the surface. (You won't be able to get in much more than a top and bottom ribbon in a large baking pan; just distribute the swirl as best you can.) Drag a spatula or butter knife through the swirled ice cream just once or twice if you feel it needs more ribboning, but don't get hung up on distributing everything perfectly: As you scoop the ice cream, drag the scoop across the surface rather than plunging it in and you will be rewarded with a pretty swirl, even if you didn't perfectly layer in the swirl when you packed it.

You can also dress up sandwiches for the dinner table by spreading a sauce onto cookie bottoms before sandwiching or by serving each guest a small bowl of sauce warmed to dipping consistency for dipping their sandwich as they eat. Any of the swirls, ripples, ribbons, or coatings will work in this role.

Fudge Ripple GF
MAKES ABOUT 1 CUP (240 ML)

This smooth ripple forms rich tunnels of fudge that stay chewy-soft even after the ice cream freezes. For deep dark chocolate flavor, use Valrhona cocoa and 70% chocolate.

½ cup (120 ml) heavy cream

¼ cup (60 ml) golden syrup, inverted sugar syrup (page 27), or agave nectar

3 tablespoons unsweetened Dutch-processed cocoa powder

3 ounces (85 g) extra-bittersweet chocolate (64 to 72 percent cacao), chopped

½ teaspoon pure vanilla extract

¼ teaspoon kosher salt

Whisk the cream, syrup, and cocoa powder in a medium saucepan to completely incorporate the cocoa. Stir in 2 tablespoons of water.

Bring the mixture to a full, rolling boil over medium heat, then remove from the heat and drop in the chocolate. Let stand a minute or two for the chocolate to melt, then stir until smooth. Stir in the vanilla and salt. Cool to room temperature before swirling into ice cream. If not using immediately, refrigerate in an airtight container for up to 2 weeks.

For dipping, warm gently in a microwave oven or in a saucepan over medium heat, stirring frequently, just until warm.

VARIATION: Mocha Ripple
Substitute a shot (2 tablespoons) of strong, freshly brewed espresso for the 2 tablespoons of water.

Salty Caramel Swirl GF
MAKES ABOUT 1⅓ CUPS (320 ML)

Salt compounds caramel's complexity and tempers its bitter edge. I take this caramel to a very dark level by heating the sugar until it threatens to burn, encouraged by the maven of ice cream, sauces, and all things sweet, David Lebovitz. If you have not made caramel before, or are uncomfortable flirting with fate, the caramel is perfectly delicious when cooked to a dark amber, nowhere near burnt. A light-colored saucepan will allow you to more easily observe the changes in color as the sugar caramelizes—watch it carefully, as the process can go quickly. While caramel is not at all difficult to make, do take care—the sugar rises far above the temperature of boiling water. Protect yourself with heavy oven mitts, add cream at arm's length to avoid steam and splashing, and stir with a long-handled wooden spoon or heatproof spatula.

1 cup (240 ml) heavy cream

¾ cup (150 g) granulated sugar

¼ cup (60 ml) golden syrup
or inverted sugar syrup (page 27)

2 tablespoons unsalted butter, cold,
cut into 8 pieces

½ teaspoon pure vanilla extract

½ teaspoon medium-grind sea salt, such as
gray salt, fleur de sel, or Maldon sea salt

Heat the cream in a small saucepan just until it is warm; set aside off the heat.

Stir together the sugar, golden syrup, and 2 tablespoons of water in a large heavy saucepan over medium heat to wet all of the sugar. Without stirring, cook until the mixture reaches a simmer, then reduce the heat to low, cover, and simmer for 3 minutes. Remove the cover, raise the heat to medium-high, and boil vigorously without stirring (swirl the pan as needed for even cooking) until the caramel turns a deep amber or a bit darker, 8 to 10 minutes longer, watching carefully to avoid burning it.

Remove from the heat and, standing back to avoid spatters that can burn, carefully pour in the warm cream in a slow, steady stream, which will cause a great deal of fury in the pan. When the excitement subsides, return the pan to medium heat and stir with a wooden spoon or heatproof spatula to melt and smooth any pieces of hardened caramel.

Transfer the caramel to a heatproof bowl and stir in the butter, two pieces at a time, until it is fully incorporated. Stir in the vanilla and salt. Let

cool completely before swirling into ice cream. If not using immediately, refrigerate the caramel in an airtight container for up to 2 weeks.

For dipping, warm the caramel gently in a microwave oven, or in a saucepan over medium heat, stirring frequently, just until warm.

VARIATION: Espresso Caramel Swirl

Reduce the cream to ¾ cup (180 ml) and stir 2 shots (¼ cup / 60 ml) of freshly brewed espresso, or 2 teaspoons instant espresso granules dissolved in ¼ cup (60 ml) water, into the cream warming in the saucepan. If the caramel is thin after adding the liquid, boil a few minutes longer until thickened. Omit the butter. No need to take the sugar beyond a deep amber for this one—the coffee contributes its own enticingly bitter flavors.

Dulce de Leche GF
MAKES ABOUT 1¼ CUPS (300 ML)

Cooking milk with sugar transforms it into a rich, sticky, gooey confection that is perfect for spreading on ice cream sandwiches, or to flavor Dulce de Leche Ice Cream (page 95). Baking soda isn't essential, but it helps to achieve a rich, dark color. The milk is the most important ingredient—the reason for making this from scratch rather than starting with sweetened condensed milk from a can. Choose good-quality milk that has not been ultrapasteurized, and be sure to cook it low and slow. When made with goat's milk, the sweet goes by the name *cajeta*, and is equally delicious.

Use a light-colored pot to more easily note the color change as the milk and sugar caramelize.

½ teaspoon baking soda

1 quart (960 ml) whole milk

½ cup (100 g) granulated sugar

¼ cup packed (50 g) light brown sugar

2 tablespoons golden syrup, inverted sugar syrup (page 27), or agave nectar

1 vanilla bean, split

½ teaspoon kosher salt

Dissolve the baking soda in 2 teaspoons of water; set aside by the stove.

Whisk the milk, granulated and brown sugars, and golden syrup in a large, deep, heavy nonreactive soup pot over medium heat to dissolve the sugar. Use the tip of a paring knife to scrape the seeds from the vanilla bean into the milk; drop in the pod too. Bring to a simmer, reduce the heat to low, and cover the pot for 5 minutes to help dissolve any sugar clinging to the sides. Remove the cover.

Add the baking soda mixture, taking care to avoid boil-overs and steam burns, as the mixture will bubble up fiercely. The mixture will continue to foam as you cook it. (If the foam climbs too close to the top at any point, take the pot off the heat briefly, stir, and return to the heat.)

Simmer the mixture slowly, stirring frequently with a wooden spoon or heatproof spatula, as the milk goes from white, to light tan, to a medium and then a deep caramel color. It's ready when it thickens to the texture of a caramel sauce and measures about 1¼ cups (300 ml), about 1 hour. (It will thicken further as it cools.)

Stir in the salt and let cool to room temperature. Remove the vanilla pod; rinse and save for another use (see page 26), or discard.

If not using immediately, refrigerate the dulce de leche in a clean glass jar, covered, for up to 1 month.

Balsamic "Fudge" Ripple GF DF
MAKES ½ CUP (120 ML)

I once had the opportunity to taste hundred-year-old *aceto balsamico tradizionale*—the traditional balsamico of Modena, Italy, made by aging cooked grape must in a series of wood casks. We climbed to the attic of the *acetaia*, where the producer dipped his cup into the cask to retrieve a syrup as thick as fudge, and even more flavorful. If you have twenty-five-year or older balsamico on hand, swirl that into your ice cream as-is. I've devised this alternative, which tastes fudgy without chocolate, and is rich, complex, and considerably less costly than the most expensive balsamic.

Use a good-quality balsamic vinegar—such as Fini, Giusti, or Lucini—and a young, fruity table wine without much oak or tannin. Sweet wines work well too, but reduce the syrup by 1 tablespoon to adjust for their added sweetness.

½ cup (120 ml) balsamic vinegar

¼ cup (60 ml) golden syrup, inverted sugar syrup (page 27), or agave nectar

2 tablespoons dry red wine (such as a Zinfandel, Grenache, or Merlot), or additional balsamic vinegar

¼ teaspoon kosher salt

Stir the vinegar, syrup, wine, and salt in a heavy, nonreactive medium saucepan over medium heat until the mixture simmers. Reduce the heat to simmer gently, stirring occasionally, until the sauce is syrupy and reduced by almost half, 12 to 15 minutes. Cool to room temperature before swirling into ice cream. (The sauce will thicken further as it cools.)

Berry Ribbon Two Ways GF DF

MAKES ABOUT ⅔ CUP (160 ML), DEPENDING ON THE TYPE OF BERRIES

Sweetening berries, then evaporating and thickening some of their liquid, produces a colorful ribbon that remains soft when frozen. Blueberries won't need to be strained, as their seeds are not as prominent.

2 cups (about 300 g) raspberries, blackberries, blueberries, or other berries

6 tablespoons (75 g) granulated sugar

1 teaspoon fresh lemon juice

Stir the berries with the sugar in a saucepan over medium heat until they soften and become very juicy, about 5 minutes.

Puree the mixture with an immersion blender in the pot (beware of splatters—they stain!), or transfer to a blender or food processor and puree.

Pass the berries through a standard- or fine-mesh strainer into a bowl, stirring and pressing until only the seeds remain; discard the seeds. Return the syrup to the saucepan and simmer until syrupy and reduced to about ⅔ cup (160 ml), 5 to 8 minutes. Stir in the lemon juice. Cool completely, then refrigerate in an airtight container until cold.

For a chunkier ribbon, omit the lemon juice, reduce the sugar to ¼ cup (50 g), and add 2 tablespoons Framboise or raspberry wine along with the berries and sugar. Skip the blending and straining steps, and use a flexible spatula to smash the fruit as you heat and reduce the mixture to about 1 cup (240 ml).

Cherry Swirl GF DF

MAKES ABOUT 1 CUP (240 ML)

Use with either sweet or tart cherries, but with the latter, increase the sugar by 2 tablespoons or to taste. (I love 'em tart!)

2 teaspoons tapioca starch

2 teaspoons fresh lemon juice

2 cups (300 g) pitted sweet cherries, fresh or frozen and thawed

2 tablespoons granulated sugar

Pinch of salt

Stir the tapioca and lemon juice in a small bowl to dissolve the tapioca; set near the stove.

Stir the cherries, sugar, and salt in a medium nonreactive saucepan over medium heat until the cherries burst, exude their juices, and soften, about 5 minutes. Stir the lemon juice mixture, then scrape into the cherries and cook, stirring constantly, until the mixture thickens, about 90 seconds. Taste and add more sugar or lemon juice if you wish.

Use an immersion blender or food processor to puree the mixture, leaving it a little bit chunky. (Beware: Cherries stain!)

Let cool to room temperature, then cover and refrigerate until cold.

Lemon Curd GF DF

MAKES 1 CUP (240 ML)

Used in the Lemon Zinger (page 77), this sweet-tangy curd is also wonderful ribboned into other ice creams, or spread on cookies

when sandwiching. Pairing chocolate and lemon is a love-it or hate-it proposition; I'm in the love-it camp. If you are too, try swirling lemon curd into Milk Gelato (page 114) and encasing it in Soft Chocolate Cookie Bars (page 31) for a modern spin on Pure Nostalgia. Or spread a dollop on the meringue cookies when filling the Berry Pavlova (page 71) to back up the lemon verbena in the Blackberry-Buttermilk ice cream.

1 large egg

2 large egg yolks

⅔ cup (134 g) granulated sugar

⅓ cup (80 ml) fresh lemon juice

1 teaspoon finely grated lemon zest

¼ teaspoon kosher salt

Set a fine-mesh strainer over a small bowl and place it near the stove.

Whisk the egg, yolks, sugar, lemon juice and zest, and salt in a heavy, nonreactive saucepan until well mixed. Gently heat the mixture over low heat, stirring constantly with a heatproof spatula (be sure to get into the corners), until the curd thickly coats a spoon drawn through it, 6 to 8 minutes.

Scrape the curd into the strainer, then press it through the strainer into the bowl. Set the bowl of curd into a larger bowl of ice and water and stir occasionally until cool, taking care not to slosh water into the bowl.

Once cool, refrigerate the curd in an airtight container for up to 1 week.

Chocolate-Hazelnut Spread GF DF

MAKES ABOUT ¾ CUP (180 ML)

This spread gets its rich, chocolaty flavor from cocoa, so it's worth splurging on a full-flavored brand, such as Valrhona or Guittard. If you have it on hand, hazelnut oil reinforces the nutty flavor. Be patient in making the paste: Unless you are working with a heavy-duty blender, it will take time. I'm not as fond of the coarser spread that results from using a food processor, but if your taste in nut butters runs more to chunky than creamy, give it a whirl. In addition to the Chocolate-Hazelnut Ice Cream on page 47, the spread is wonderful slathered on cookies before sandwiching them with ice cream. It's tasty on a spoon straight from the jar, too.

1 cup (132 g) hazelnuts

1 tablespoon hazelnut oil or neutral vegetable oil, or more as needed

¼ teaspoon kosher salt, plus more to taste

½ cup (60 g) powdered sugar

3 tablespoons unsweetened Dutch-processed cocoa powder, plus more to taste

¼ teaspoon pure vanilla extract

Preheat the oven to 325°F (165°C). Spread the nuts on a rimmed baking sheet and toast until they are quite dark—even just beginning to smoke, about 20 minutes. Rub the nuts vigorously in a clean dish towel to remove most of the skins.

Pour 1 tablespoon of oil into a blender jar and add the warm hazelnuts and the salt. Process to make a paste, scraping down the jar as needed to keep the nuts moving. Continue processing for several minutes longer to make as smooth a paste as your blender will allow, adding more oil if needed. Add the sugar, cocoa powder, and vanilla; process until well blended, about a minute longer. Taste and add more cocoa powder or salt if you wish.

Refrigerate the spread in an airtight container for up to 4 weeks. Let stand at room temperature for 15 minutes to soften before using.

Mix-ins

Add mix-ins during the last minute of spinning the ice cream. Most machines have a feed tube to facilitate this, though some are small and awkward to use. If that's the case, use an ice cream paddle or flexible spatula to fold them in as you transfer the ice cream to its freezer container.

To mix ingredients into store-bought ice cream, soften the ice cream slightly (about 20 minutes at room temperature), then transfer it to a bowl and use a spatula to gently stir or swirl in the ingredients. To thoroughly mix a flavoring into ice cream, put the softened ice cream in a stand mixer and use the paddle attachment to mix it. Whatever your method, avoid letting the ice cream melt any more than needed, as it will become slightly icier with each melting and refreezing.

Stracciatella

Make your ice cream *stracciatella* style—a technique where chocolate is melted with a bit of oil, cooled, then drizzled into the spinning ice cream in the machine during the last minute of processing. The chocolate hardens as it hits the cold ice cream, while the dasher breaks it into shards that melt smoothly on the tongue—a decidedly more sensual experience than crunching on frozen chocolate chips. You can achieve the same effect by drizzling and folding in the chocolate as you pack the ice cream into its container. (See Chocolate Chip Ice Cream, page 53, for a detailed recipe.)

Fruit

To prevent icy pieces of berries or other fruit from marring your creamy treat, cut fruits into small pieces (remove pits, seeds, and skins) and put them into a bowl. Sprinkle with 2 to 3 tablespoons of sugar per cup of fruit (depending on the tartness of your fruit), stir and smash the fruit with a fork, and let stand at room temperature for about 30 minutes, until the fruit exudes much of its juices. (For firmer fruits like peaches, cherries, or plums, cook the diced fruit with the sugar for a few minutes to soften.) Drain off the juice (save for ice cream toppings or your morning yogurt), or cook it briefly with 1½ teaspoons of tapioca starch per ½ cup (120 ml) of liquid to make a thickened syrup. Add a few drops of lemon juice for brightness, if you wish.

If you are using the fruit only (no syrup), add it during the last minute of spinning in your ice cream machine. If using the fruit with its thickened syrup, fold it into the ice cream as you would a swirl.

Nuts, Brittles, Morsels, and Marshmallows

Stir in chopped nuts or nut brittle, toffee, or chocolate chips during the last minute of spinning the ice cream in your machine, or use an ice cream paddle or flexible spatula to fold them in as you transfer the ice cream to its freezer container.

Maple-Buttered Pecans GF

MAKES 1 CUP (150 G)

Created for the Pumpkin-Pecan Ice Cream (page 145), these toasty, maple-scented nuts enriched with butter are perfect for folding into a variety of ice creams, or rolling onto the sides of sandwiches. Their flavor screams "autumn," but they are equally good at any time of year.

1 tablespoon unsalted butter

1 cup (120 g) pecans, coarsely chopped

2 tablespoons maple sugar or brown sugar

¼ teaspoon medium-grind sea salt, such as gray salt, fleur de sel, or Maldon sea salt, or more to taste

Melt the butter in a medium skillet over medium heat. Add the pecans and cook, stirring frequently, until they smell toasty and turn light golden, taking care not to burn them. Off the heat, sprinkle the sugar and salt evenly over the nuts and stir with a heatproof spatula until the sugar melts, returning the pan to the heat if needed to glaze the nuts. Transfer the nuts to a silicone baking mat or a sheet of parchment paper to cool completely. Once cooled, chop or break apart the nuts if they have clustered.

Honey-Roasted Peanut Brittle GF DF

MAKES ABOUT 2 CUPS (220 G)

These sweet, crunchy nuts are terrific rolled around any peanut-friendly sandwich, and are a natural for the Top Banana (page 92). Watch the brittle carefully as you cook it: Once the browning begins, it can quickly burn.

1 cup (140 g) roasted peanuts

¼ cup (84 g) mild-flavored honey

Pinch of fleur de sel, gray salt, or fine sea salt, if the peanuts are not salted

Line a baking sheet with parchment paper or a silicone baking mat.

Use a heatproof spatula to stir the peanuts, honey, and 1 tablespoon water in a nonstick skillet over medium-high heat until the mixture browns, about 2 minutes.

Without delay, scrape the hot mixture onto the prepared pan, spreading it out as best you can. If you did not use salted peanuts, sprinkle the warm brittle with a pinch of salt, scattering it from high above to distribute the salt evenly over the surface. Let the brittle cool completely.

Pulse the brittle in a food processor, or chop it with a sharp, heavy knife, until it is in pieces about the size of a peanut.

Almond Crack GF DF

MAKES 1 GENEROUS CUP (160 G)

The math is simple: Sugar + salt = addictive. Caramelized sugar + salt = very addictive. Caramelized sugar + salt + almonds = crack. But you don't need to be a math whiz to enjoy these addictive nuts, which you will be tempted to eat by the handful. Just be sure to save some for rolling sandwiches or folding into ice cream.

Watch these carefully as you cook them—they may smoke and threaten to burn, and are best when cooked dark but short of burning. These can also be made with other nuts, such as walnuts or pecans.

1 cup (140 g) almonds, blanched or not, coarsely chopped

3 tablespoons granulated sugar

¼ teaspoon medium-grind sea salt, such as gray salt, fleur de sel, or Maldon sea salt, or more to taste

Toast the almonds in a medium skillet over medium heat, watching carefully, until they begin to smell toasty and turn lightly golden. Sprinkle the sugar and salt over them and continue to cook, stirring with a heatproof spatula or wooden spoon, until the sugar melts and turns a dark caramel color, about a minute.

Spread the nuts in a single layer on a silicone baking mat or a sheet of parchment paper. Let cool completely, then break up any clusters with your hands.

Ginger Crumble

MAKES ABOUT 1 CUP (140 G)

Used to dress up the Rhubarb Crumble sandwich (page 60), this crumble is a nice addition to any sandwich where a bit of buttery crunch and a ginger zing are in order. To vary the flavor, substitute a different spice for the ginger, such as ground cinnamon or cardamom. Use old-fashioned or quick-style oats, but not instant.

¼ cup (33 g) unbleached all-purpose flour

¼ cup (30 g) rolled oats

¼ cup packed (50 g) light brown sugar

1 teaspoon ground ginger

¼ teaspoon kosher salt

¼ teaspoon pure vanilla extract

2 tablespoons unsalted butter, softened

2 tablespoons sliced almonds (optional)

Stir together the flour, oats, brown sugar, ginger, and salt in a bowl. Sprinkle the vanilla evenly over the mixture, then scatter on the butter. Using your fingertips, rub in the butter until the mixture looks like clumpy sand. Scatter the almonds over the top, if using, and mix them in with your fingers. Refrigerate for 30 minutes.

Preheat the oven to 375°F (190°C) with a rack in the center of the oven. Line a rimmed baking sheet with parchment paper or a silicone baking mat.

Use your fingers to crumble the topping mixture onto the baking sheet. Bake until golden, 10 to 12 minutes, stirring and turning with a spatula once or twice during baking. Let the crumble cool completely.

Break up any large clumps with your fingers before using to roll sandwiches. Refrigerate leftover crumble in an airtight container for up to 1 week.

Vanilla-Scented Marshmallows GF DF

MAKES 25 LARGE MARSHMALLOWS

I learned this sweet technique from pastry chef Marisa Churchill when I assisted her with her book *Sweet & Skinny*.

If making the marshmallows for the S'mores sandwich (page 123), you will have more than you need, but it's not practical to make less. Quarter any remaining marsh-mallows (or cut smaller if you wish)—they're great to have on hand to fold into ice cream, top sundaes, or enjoy on their own.

2 tablespoons powdered sugar, plus more for tossing

1 tablespoon unflavored gelatin powder

¾ cup (150 g) granulated sugar

2 large egg whites

¼ teaspoon cream of tartar

Pinch of salt

¼ teaspoon pure vanilla extract

Line a 9-inch (23-cm) square pan with parchment paper, with the ends extending up the sides on all four sides. Sift 1 tablespoon of powdered sugar over the bottom of the pan to prevent sticking.

Put 2 tablespoons of water in the bowl of a stand mixer fitted with the whisk attachment and sprinkle the gelatin evenly over the surface, making sure all of the gelatin is moistened.

Stir the granulated sugar with ¼ cup (60 ml) water in a small saucepan, then cook over medium-low heat without stirring until the sugar dissolves and the mixture is clear. Cover the pan for 3 minutes to help dissolve any sugar crystals on the side of the pan, then remove the cover, clip on a candy thermometer, and boil until the syrup reaches 238°F (115°C; soft ball stage), about 5 minutes.

When the syrup is at about 230°F (110°C), stir the gelatin in the mixer bowl with a fork or whisk to break it up (it will not have dissolved completely), then add the egg whites, cream of tartar, and salt. Beat on low speed until frothy, scraping the bowl to ensure that the gelatin mixes completely with the egg whites.

When the syrup reaches 238°F (115°C), with the mixer on low, carefully drizzle the syrup down the side of the bowl in a slow, steady thread, avoiding the beater to prevent splattering. (Handle the syrup with care, as it will be very hot.) When all the sugar is in, increase the speed to medium-high and beat until the whites form stiff peaks and the bottom of the bowl feels barely warm to the touch, about 5 minutes. Add the vanilla during the last minute of beating.

Use an offset spatula to spread the marshmallow evenly into the prepared pan. Let stand uncovered for 2 hours, then sift 1 tablespoon of powdered sugar over the top. Cut the marshmallow in 5 strips in each direction to make 25 marshmallows.

Toss with powdered sugar in a bowl to keep them from getting sticky, then store in an airtight container at room temperature for up to 1 week.

Roll-'ems

Roll the edges of your sandwiches for textural contrast and a pretty finish. To aid in adhering the topping, roll sandwiches shortly after filling them, while the ice cream is soft. Put the topping in a wide, shallow bowl. Hold and turn the sandwich over the bowl with one hand while using the other to pick up and gently press handfuls of topping onto the sides of the sandwich. Serve immediately, or return the sandwiches to the freezer until firm. You can use these same toppings with the Chocolate Shell—press your dipped sandwiches in the topping while the shell is still soft and refrigerate at least 15 minutes to set the shell.

Use almost any of the recipes for homemade mix-ins (pages 161–164) as roll-'ems, or see the Optional Embellishments column in **Sandwich It Your Way!** (page 166) for additional inspiration.

Coatings

Dip a filled sandwich partially or fully in Chocolate Shell and let it harden for a treat reminiscent of childhood. Press on additional decorations for added flair. For a black and white tuxedo coating, dip half of each sandwich in dark chocolate and the other half in white chocolate. (See Auld Lang Syne, page 151.)

Chocolate Shell GF DF

MAKES ENOUGH TO HALF-DIP ABOUT 12 SAND-WICHES OR FULLY COAT 6 TO 8 SANDWICHES

This chocolate coating could not be easier. A bit of oil keeps the chocolate smooth for dipping, then magically helps it to harden to a brittle coating in only a few minutes in the freezer. The elegant chocolate layer shatters beautifully when you bite into the sandwich, melting smoothly on the tongue.

I prefer an extra-bittersweet chocolate for this—64 to 72 percent cacao—but choose whatever chocolate you like, from milk to dark. For a white chocolate shell, increase the oil to ¼ cup (60 ml), and choose a good-quality white chocolate, such as El Rey, Ghirardelli, or Guittard (not chips).

The sandwiches should be firmly frozen before dipping. To decorate the sandwiches, press chopped and toasted nuts, coconut, sprinkles, or other decorations onto the dipped sandwiches before the chocolate firms. Any remaining Chocolate Shell can be melted and served over ice cream, or can be stirred into ice cream as it spins for a stracciatella (chocolate chip) effect (see page 161).

1 pound (454 g) chocolate, chopped

3 tablespoons neutral vegetable oil or coconut oil

Choose a metal bowl (for the stovetop) or microwave-safe bowl that is deep enough to submerge a sandwich and wide enough to easily dip into. (For the microwave, a 4-cup / 1-L glass measuring cup works well.)

Melt the chocolate with the oil in a double boiler or bowl placed over, but not touching, about an inch (2½ cm) of simmering water in a saucepan. Alternatively, melt the chocolate with the oil in the microwave until you can stir it smooth. You do not need to get the chocolate very hot—just warm enough to melt when you stir it. Set aside until the chocolate is just barely warm and still smooth and fluid.

To dip the sandwiches, have a parchment-lined baking sheet in the freezer and the melted chocolate close at hand. (If it becomes too firm to dip, gently warm the chocolate until fluid.)

Dunk a sandwich into the chocolate to coat half or all of the sandwich, using a small offset spatula as an aid to paint on the chocolate and scrape off any excess. Transfer the sandwich to the baking sheet in the freezer. Repeat to coat the remaining sandwiches. Freeze until the chocolate sets, about 15 minutes, before individually wrapping the sandwiches or layering them between sheets of parchment or waxed paper in an airtight container.

SANDWICH IT YOUR WAY!

This book shares my carefully curated collection of ice cream sandwiches, but I hope it will also be the launching point for your own creations. This chart is meant to get your imagination spinning on the infinite variations you might create, using the recipes in this book as well as other homemade and store-bought ice creams, holders, and embellishments.

To get started, choose a filling from the first column and a holder from the second. Put them together and you've got a sandwich custom made to your own taste. You don't have to stop there—consider enhancements from the last column, which may be mixed into the ice creams, spread on cookie bottoms before sandwiching, rolled around the sides, or used as a dipping sauce. You'll want to chop any large chunks into bite-size pieces for folding in or rolling sandwich sides.

May all your sandwiches elicit screams of delight!

1 CHOOSE AN ICE CREAM, YOGURT OR SORBET

FRUITY

Apricot Ice Cream

Apricot Sorbet

Blueberry Sorbet

Cherry Cheesecake Ice Cream

Orange Sherbet

Peaches and Cream Ice Cream

Raspberry Swirl Ice Cream

Rhubarb Ice Cream

TANGY

Blackberry-Buttermilk Ice Cream

Frozen Honey-Vanilla Goat's Milk

Key Lime Ice Cream

Lemon Curd Ice Cream

Plum Frozen Yogurt

Strawberry-Balsamic Frozen Yogurt

MILKY

Cream Cheese Ice Cream

Milk Gelato

Vanilla Bean Frozen Custard

Vanilla Ice Cream

NUTTY

Coconut Sorbet

Peanut Butter Ice Cream

Pistachio Gelato

Toasted Almond Ice Cream

EXOTIC

Caribbean Banana Ice Cream

Date Sorbet

Jasmine Ice Cream

Kaffir Lime and Lemongrass Sorbet

Piña Colada Sorbet

Rosewater Ice Cream

White Corn and Red Raspberry Ice Cream

COFFEE, BOOZE & CARAMEL

Boozy Pumpkin-Pecan Ice Cream

Champagne-Caramel Swirl Ice Cream

Dulce de Leche Ice Cream

Espresso Caramel Swirl Ice Cream

Vietnamese Coffee Ice Cream

CHOCOLATE

Chocolate Chip Ice Cream

Chocolate-Hazelnut Ice Cream

Fudge Ripple Ice Cream

Mint Chocolate Chip Ice Cream

Spicy Mexican Chocolate Ice Cream

2 PICK A HOLDER

3 CONSIDER OPTIONAL EMBELLISHMENTS

CRISPY & CRUNCHY COOKIES

Almond Wafers

Graham Crackers

Brown Sugar Oat Cakes

Maple Leaf Cookies

Shortcrust Cookies

Sugar Cone Cookies

Sugar Cookies

Vanilla Cookies

Vanilla-Orange Wafers

SOFT & CHEWY COOKIES

Almond Tea Cakes

Chocolate Sweethearts

Five-Spice Cookies

Oatmeal Cookies

Peanut Butter Cookies

Soft Chocolate Cookie Bars

Soft Ginger Cookies

Warm Chocolate Chip Cookies

CAKEY COOKIES

Blueberry Muffin Top Cookies

Carrot Cake Cookies

Snickerdoodles

BROWNIES & BARS

Brown Butter Blondies

Brown Sugar–Walnut Bars

Fudge or Espresso Fudge Brownies

SHORTBREADS & SANDIES

Black Pepper Cookies

Cornmeal Cookies

Hazelnut Sandies

Lavender-Walnut Shortbread

Macadamia Cookies

Pistachio-Cardamom Sandies

MERINGUES

Chocolate-Coconut Macaroons

Cinnamon Macarons

Crispy-Chewy Meringues

Parisian Cocoa Macarons

OUT THERE

Banana or zucchini bread*

Brioche Bun

Coffee cake slices*

Cookie Dough

Cream puffs or profiterole shells*

Croissants*

Donuts or donut holes*

French toast*

Hot Dog Bun

Muffin tops*

Toast

Sliced bread*

Waffles*

SWIRLS, RIBBONS & DIPPERS

Balsamic "Fudge" Ripple

Berry Ribbon Two Ways

Espresso Caramel Swirl

Fudge Ripple

Mocha Ripple

Salty Caramel Swirl

SPREADS

Chocolate-Hazelnut Spread

Dulce de Leche

Lemon Curd

NUTS & CRUMBLES

Almond Crack

Chopped chocolate-covered almonds*

Coconut, toasted or not

Ginger Crumble

Honey-Roasted Peanut Brittle

Maple-Buttered Pecans

Other nut brittles*

Toasted, chopped nuts

FRUITS

Candied citrus peels*

Caramelized Banana

Dehydrated fruit*

Dried fruit*

Fruit mix-ins

Fruit syrups

CHIPS, MORSELS & CANDIES

Candied flower petals*

Chocolate chips or mini chocolate chips*

Chopped or crushed candies*

Colored sprinkles, jimmies, or coarse sugar*

Crystallized ginger*

Stracciatella

Chocolate-covered espresso beans*

Chocolate shavings*

Toffee, butterscotch, cinnamon, or peanut butter morsels*

OTHER MIX-INS & ROLL-'EMS

Breakfast cereal*

Crushed cookies*

Crushed pretzels*

Granola*

Vanilla-Scented Marshmallows

COATINGS

Dark Chocolate Shell

White Chocolate Shell

Tuxedo Coating

* = recipe not in book

Sources and Resources

Below are some of my preferred brands for ingredients and equipment used in the book.

Flours, grains, starches, and general baking ingredients

Bob's Red Mill
www.bobsredmill.com
Wide selection of flours, grains, sugars, spices, and other products, including tapioca starch and stone-ground blue cornmeal, as well as baking equipment.

King Arthur Flour
www.kingarthurflour.com
Information about baking, as well as graham flour, tapioca starch, maple sugar, and other baking ingredients and equipment.

Let's Do . . . Organic Tapioca Starch
www.edwardandsons.com
Ground from the cassava root in Thailand, packed in the U.S., and distributed by Edward & Sons Trading Co., Inc., this is the tapioca starch (aka tapioca flour) I generally use.

Trader Joe's
www.traderjoes.com
Excellent plain, whole milk Greek yogurt, wide variety of nuts, almond meal, maple sugar, and other ingredients, as well as powdered sugar made with tapioca rather than cornstarch. Note that items stocked may vary regionally, seasonally, and over time.

Chocolate and cocoa

Callebaut
www.barry-callebaut.com
Good-quality, widely available chocolate.

Guittard
www.guittard.com
Excellent chocolate and cocoa—the ones I reach for more than any other.

Madécasse
www.madecasse.com
Vanilla and chocolate products, including ground whole vanilla bean powder, made with a "beyond fair trade" model that aims to sustain the full chocolate production process in Madagascar.

Valrhona
www.valrhona.com
Outstanding chocolate and cocoa.

Coconut milk and coconut beverage

Less rich and dense than the canned milk, non-dairy coconut beverages are available in shelf-stable (or sometimes refrigerated) aseptic boxes, similar to soy and almond milks.

Chaokoh and Mae Ploy Coconut Milk (canned)
www.tcc-chaokoh.com

Coconut Dream Coconut Beverage (shelf-stable)
www.tastethedream.com

So Delicious Coconut Beverage (shelf-stable or refrigerated)
www.sodeliciousdairyfree.com

Dairy

Karoun Dairies
www.karouncheese.com
Producer of my favorite labne, labeled Mediterranean-Style Labne Kefir Cheese.

Straus Family Creamy
www.strausfamilycreamery.com
Excellent whole milk yogurt. This is the brand I often use to make the strained yogurt used in many of the ice creams. (See page 27.)

Spices, sweeteners, flavorings, and oils

Carlo Beverage Enterprises / Lebanese Arak Corp (LAC)
www.lacproducts.com
Lebanese flavorings and beverages, including rosewater.

Cortas
www.usacortas.com
Lebanese flavorings, including rosewater.

Frontier Natural Products Coop
www.frontiercoop.com
Organic oils and flavoring extracts, as well as herbs and spices.

La Tourangelle
www.latourangelle.com
Artisanal nut, seed, and other oils.

LorAnn Oils
www.lorannoils.com
Flavorings, essential oils, fragrances, and specialty ingredients, including natural peppermint oil. Super Strength Flavors are available in sizes of one dram and up. Also sanding sugars for adding shimmer to your cookie tops.

Lyle's Golden Syrup
www.lylesgoldensyrup.com
The only brand of golden syrup I have found or used, this British product is often located in the ethnic foods aisle, packed in tins or plastic bottles.

Penzeys Spices
www.penzeys.com
Wide range of quality herbs, spices, and extracts, as well as high-butterfat cocoas, both Dutch-processed and natural.

Spicely Organic Spices
www.spicely.com
Good-quality herbs and spices, often available at supermarkets, including many Whole Foods locations.

The Vanilla Company
www.vanilla.com
Fair trade, sustainably produced vanilla beans, powder, extract, and paste, as well as a great deal of information about vanilla and how it is produced, sold, and used.

General equipment and supplies

Sur la Table
www.surlatable.com
Ice cream machines, scoops, molds, decorations, mixes, and a variety of related equipment and supplies.

Williams-Sonoma
www.williams-sonoma.com
Ice cream machines, scoops, molds, decorations, mixes, and a variety of related equipment and supplies.

Baking mats

Matfer (Exopat)
www.matfer.com

Silpat
www.silpat.com

Ice cream machines

Cuisinart
www.cuisinart.com

KitchenAid
www.kitchenaid.com

Whynter
www.whynter.com

Ice cream sandwich molds

Cuisipro
www.cuisipro.com
Makes a Mini Ice Cream Sandwich Maker that can be used to cut and build mini sandwiches in a heart, star, or circle shape. The Ice Cream Scoop & Stack scoops up ice cream and presses it out into neat 2-inch (5-cm) disks.

NorPro
www.norpro.com
Makes an Ice Cream Sandwich Maker for building sandwiches in a rectangular mold, as well as a variety of scoops, graters, strainers, and other kitchen equipment.

Tovolo
www.tovolo.com
Maker of the molds used in this book, which come in three sets of three shapes each: Classic Icons, Farm Animals, and Holiday Shapes. Williams-Sonoma and Bed Bath & Beyond sell branded versions of these or similar molds.

Wilton
www.wilton.com
Makes a 12-Cavity Ice Cream Sandwich Pan in rectangular or round shapes with a nifty waffle surface, as well as a variety of cookie cutters and decorations that could be used to make sandwiches.

For more information on ice cream, baking, and general dessert technique

The number of websites and blogs with recipes and cooking information seems to grow exponentially each day. The following are but a few sites where I have found inspiration or information on ice cream sandwich–related ingredients and techniques.

www.alicemedrich.blogspot.com

www.baking911.com

www.betterbaking.com

www.chezpim.typepad.com/blogs

www.chocolateandzucchini.com

www.curiouscook.com

www.davidlebovitz.com

www.eggbeater.typepad.com

www.epicurious.com

www.exploratorium.edu/cooking

www.joyofbaking.com

www.101cookbooks.com

www.smittenkitchen.com

www.thekitchn.com

Bibliography

The following books and resources provided helpful guidance as I unlocked secrets to making tempting ice cream, alluring holders, and making both even more enticing as sandwiches. I've included them here in case they might help you, too.

Jeni Britton Bauer. *Jeni's Splendid Ice Creams at Home*. New York: Artisan, 2012.

Shirley O. Corriher. *BakeWise: The Hows and Whys of Successful Baking with Over 200 Magnificent Recipes*. New York: Scribner, 2008.

Shirley O. Corriher. *CookWise: The Hows and Whys of Successful Cooking, The Secrets of Cooking Revealed*. New York: William Morrow, 1997.

Kris Hoogerhyde, Anne Walker, and Dabney Gough. *Sweet Cream and Sugar Cones: 90 Recipes for Making Your Own Ice Cream and Frozen Treats from Bi-Rite Creamery*. Emeryville, CA: Ten Speed Press, 2012.

David Lebovitz. *The Perfect Scoop: Ice Creams, Sorbets, Granitas, and Sweet Accompaniments*. Emeryville, CA: Ten Speed Press, 2010.

Emily Luchetti. *A Passion for Ice Cream: 95 Recipes for Fabulous Desserts*. San Francisco: Chronicle Books, 2006.

Harold McGee. *Keys to Good Cooking: A Guide to Making the Best of Food and Recipes*. New York: The Penguin Press, 2010.

Harold McGee. *On Food and Cooking: The Science and Lore of the Kitchen*. New York: Scribner, 2004.

Jeri Quinzio. *Of Sugar and Snow: A History of Ice Cream Making*. Berkeley: University of California Press, 2009.

Laura Weiss. *Ice Cream: A Global History*. Chicago: Reaktion Books/University of Chicago Press, 2011.

Author Bio

Jennie Schacht has authored and co-authored several books, among them *Farmers' Market Desserts*, the forthcoming *Southern Italian Desserts* (with Rosetta Costantino), and *The Wine Lover's Dessert Cookbook* (with Mary Cech). She has consulted to numerous chefs, restaurateurs, and authors on developing their book concepts and proposals. Her culinary and health care consulting company, Schacht & Associates, has raised over $135 million for public and not-for-profit organizations.

Jennie lives in Oakland, California, and was 2006 president of the San Francisco Professional Food Society. Look for updates, event information, errata, and additional recipes at www.i-scream-sandwich.com.

Photographer Bio

Sara Remington is an award-winning photographer based in the San Francisco Bay Area. She has photographed over 30 cookbooks, was nominated for a James Beard Award for her photography in *The Blue Chair Jam Cookbook*, and was recently featured in a 10-page spread in *Communication Arts*. Sara continues to travel the globe shooting editorial stories and high-end cookbooks, as well as maintaining a solid roster of advertising clients such as Peet's Coffee and Tea, Häagen Dazs ice cream, and President Cheese. She is in production writing and shooting her first book about childhood memories of food and travel in France, slated for a spring 2013 release. See more of Sara's work at www.sararemington.com.

ACKNOWLEDGMENTS

A cookbook may be written in a group or largely in the solitude of one's own office and kitchen, but it is always produced in community. Here I wish to acknowledge the key players, though there are undeniably as many more who helped me to nurture ideas, think them through, solve problems, master concepts, and produce this book. I love you all, and not only because I just downed two caffeine- and sugar-permeated Wake-up Call sandwiches.

I could not have dreamt up a more competent and pleasant publisher than Stewart, Tabori & Chang, nor a more attentive editor than Elinor Hutton, whose encouragement kept me marching forward on a tight and challenging schedule, and who patiently allowed me to taunt her by recapitulating tempting sandwich formulas when she was too far away to taste them. Were it not for Leslie Stoker's enthusiasm for the concept, the book might never have been brought to fruition. Ellie and Leslie were full of great ideas at every turn for making this the very best book possible. Matthew Bouloutian and Vivian Ghazarian at Modern Good created a vibrant design that perfectly conveys the spirit of the book, and copyeditor Leda Scheintaub made certain everything was in perfect order. Advance thanks go to the sales, marketing, and publicity teams for getting the word out about *i scream SANDWICH!*

I had been searching for an opportunity to work with the talented Sara Remington ever since we were introduced by my agent several years ago. Since that time, I've seen so many books brightened by her keen and artistic eye, and it's been an honor to observe her in action and have her images decorate this book. I've had the pleasure of working with stylist Kim Kissling twice before, so was thrilled when Sara suggested including her on the team. She and her assistants, Abby Stolfo and Rachel Colleen Boller, went above and beyond all reasonable expectations to make and style every last ice cream, holder, and embellishment in the book for the evocative images you see here. New to me was prop stylist Dani Fisher, but as soon as I viewed her work online I was certain she was the right person for this project. Kassandra Madeiros

ably helped with imaging and a million other things, allowing everyone to stay on task. Not only did this team produce unimaginably beautiful work, we also had a blast working together.

Carole Bidnick took me under her wing as my literary agent before I even had a project to propose to her, and she has provided stellar service with every book and between them. Carole holds an author's hand without choking it, encouraging or discouraging as appropriate, gently guiding at every step. Even when you don't agree with her, you can pretty much count on Carole turning out to be right.

I am perpetually overwhelmed by the generosity of my unflappable team of volunteer recipe testers, who approach each project with delight and deliver feedback that ensures the recipes work once they get to you. For this book, they include a few who have tested recipes for me before—Kathy Andre, Ruth Brousseau (and her merry troop of testers: Fred Brousseau, Larry and Chandra Miller, Art Lande, and Abby Snay), and Sue Burish (with Diane Waas). New to the team were Laurel Trotter (and her friend David Byron), Karen Hall and Marc Kelley, Penni Wisner, and my recently discovered cousin, Jill Warren Lucas, who turns out to share my giddiness for anything that happens in a kitchen. In addition to preparing ice creams and more for the photo shoot, Rachel Colleen Boller of Milkglass Baking (www.milkglassbaking.com) test marketed a great number of the sandwiches with customers at her farmers' market stand. Thanks to Harold McGee for helping to troubleshoot an ice cream that resisted freezing, and for shedding light on inverted sugar syrups.

A special thanks to KitchenAid for providing me with their ice cream mixer attachment to take for a spin, and likewise to Tovolo for providing molds, which have been so fun to work with.

And finally, huge thanks to my wife, Birdi, who routinely fends off outlandish book ideas tossed her way at 3:00 A.M., yet knows a winning idea when she hears one. This time, when I screamed SANDWICH!, she screamed YES!